DATE DUE			
MAY 29 1986			

THE LEWIS & CLARK TRAIL

THE LEWIS & CLARK TRAIL

ARCHIE SATTERFIELD

Illustrated by Marilyn Weber

STACKPOLE BOOKS

THE LEWIS AND CLARK TRAIL
Copyright © 1978 by
Archie Satterfield

PC

Published by   8667370
STACKPOLE BOOKS
Cameron and Kelker Streets
P.O. Box 1831
Harrisburg, Pa. 17105

First printing, April 1978
Second printing, April 1981

Published simultaneously in Don Mills, Ontario, Canada
by Thomas Nelson & Sons, Ltd.

Printed in the U.S.A.

Library of Congress Cataloging in Publication Data

Satterfield, Archie.
    The Lewis and Clark Trail.

    Includes index.
    1. Lewis and Clark Expedition. 2. Lewis and
Clark Trail. 3. Lewis, Meriwether, 1774-1809.
4. Clark, William, 1770-1818. I. Title.
F592.7.S1245 1978   917.8′04′2   77-17631
ISBN 0-8117-0935-3

To my mother
LUCILLE HOWARD SATTERFIELD

Contents

Preface

During the month we spent along the Lewis and Clark trail, there were moments that still stand out clearly in our memory; moments when the journals of the explorers took on an immediacy such that time and change were of no consequence. The journals described the scenes before us with such eloquence and good humor that we sometimes could not help but speak the words, *déjà vu*.

These moments sometimes occurred in the still hours of dawn or in midafternoon, when the sun burned the plains and dust devils swirled across the fields before dying. Sometimes we felt it late at night when the wind blew strongly and steadily, and we felt it as we neared the eastern edge of the Great Plains and tornado warnings came with the high humidity and the vague restlessness that one feels before a summer storm.

And there were the surprises, always pleasant. We expected to be bored while driving across the flatlands of eastern Montana, then south through the Dakotas but weren't. On the contrary, we found ourselves enjoying the plains as much as the mountains, but in a subtler, more subdued way.

Since there have been so many changes along the route since 1806, there were other pleasures and surprises we experienced that are totally unrelated to Lewis and Clark and their expedition and we had to learn to forget about them occasionally and partake of the present only. And that is one of the pleasures of following the trail from the Mississippi to the estuary of the Columbia: the sense of discovery that road maps and brochures do not spoil.

Following the Lewis and Clark trail is a pilgrimage every American should make at least once during his or her lifetime, and it is one that should be made in a single trip, rather than in bits and pieces. Otherwise, it is much like reading three chapters of a book, then putting it aside for a year before completing it.

This book then attempts to combine the Lewis and Clark experience during 1804–06 with the journey modern travelers can make. Only a few places remain undisturbed by the civilization that followed their trail; some rivers, or stretches of rivers, still run free, and most of the mountains remain virtually unchanged. The beauty is intact, if altered in places, and complaints against changes brought on by what we term civilization and progress are useless. What has been done can never be undone.

The explorers made a mark on the American consciousness just as surely as if they had dug an open-pit copper mine. But their mark was one of achievement under duress; it was one of devotion to duty without hope of fame or fortune. Most of all, it was duty performed in good cheer without a trace of self-pity. They were asked to do a job. They did it and then went on to other things.

Acknowledgments

Winnebago, Inc., of Forest City, Iowa, provided us with a new Itasca motorhome for exploring the Lewis and Clark Trail. It simplified the traveling immeasurably and we weren't at all embarrassed to sit in air-conditioned comfort and read of the discomfort and danger encountered by the explorers.

Kampgrounds of America (KOA) of Billings, Montana, issued us a VIP pass which was honored by most campgrounds in the system. To both KOA and the individual campground owners we are grateful. This and the use of the motorhome constitute a research grant without the paperwork and politics.

I am also indebted to my former colleagues on the Lewis and Clark Trail Advisory Commission in Washington and Oregon for tips and insights, and for displaying a remarkable degree of tolerance for some of my questions, which wouldn't have been asked had I done my homework. It is doubtful a more dedicated group of scholars will be found anywhere outside the confines of a college campus. The commissions were formed in each state along the Lewis and Clark Trail for a short-term existence.

Acknowledgments

When the term ended, the states decided to keep them in operation, and members have since served without pay or any form of reimbursement.

In addition, the state tourism information agencies were remarkably helpful on the project, and I want especially to thank those in South Dakota and Montana, both of which went beyond my initial questions and requests to give me material I did not know existed. The Forest Service in Helena, Montana, and the Bureau of Outdoor Recreation in Seattle provided reports and studies that were helpful.

The Lewis and Clark scholars, whose number is legion, will find some portions of the adventure either abbreviated or ignored entirely. I have attempted to select the events I thought most interesting, dramatic and important. I have not dwelled at length on the events surrounding the expedition, such as the Spanish attempt to prevent it, because I wanted to concentrate on the expedition itself. I consider it to be one of the great adventures in recorded history and wrote this book from that stance. Following their route today is still an adventure.

No one can write a book about Lewis and Clark without figuratively standing on the shoulders of other writers. I stood on the shoulders of Paul Russell Cutright all the way to Missouri and back to the Pacific. His magnificent book, *Lewis and Clark: Pioneering Naturalists* (University of Illinois Press. Urbana, Chicago, London 1969) is the most interesting, complete, useful to modern explorers of all the stacks of books available on the explorers. If one owned that book and the complete journals, one could be kept busy the rest of a lifetime simply enjoying them. Even the casual student of the exploration should own a set of the journals, all eight volumes and, please, not a condensed version. My set, from which all entries were taken, was published by Arno Press and cost $150 through a rare book dealer.

Finally, I must pay tribute to my family. My wife and four children enjoyed the month-long trip along the trail, and endured me while this was being written. The latter must have made them wonder occasionally if the trip had been worth it.

1
Washington to St. Louis

The Lewis and Clark Expedition of 1804–06 has so many aspects of greatness that those who write about it today are faced with a multitude of superlatives from which to choose. With time it becomes increasingly difficult both to avoid an incurable case of hero worship and to concentrate entirely on the accomplishments and consequences. Superlatives come easily — too easily perhaps — in a time when devotion to duty without complaint is not so tightly woven into the national fabric.

There may even be skeptics among us (although the author has not yet met them) who will say Lewis and Clark were simply tools of an imperialistic society. They may point out that the rapine and plundering of the land west of the Mississippi was an indirect result of the expedition. They may call Lewis and Clark the unknowing catalysts of all things unpleasant in the history of the American West.

All these charges may have their basis in fact. Those of us who view the federal government with suspicion and try to fathom motives before committing ourselves to the direction urged by leaders may consider Lewis and Clark to be incredibly naive. The inevitable question may be asked of them, "What was in it for them?" These negative aspects exist, but there is no record that Lewis or Clark considered them. They lived in an age of supreme trust and confidence in the nation's leaders, the nation's inevitable course of expansion and power. They were military men accustomed to following orders — to death, if necessary.

There is no doubt that the expedition was one of the most important events in the history of the United States. Many historians believe that it is second only to the American Revolution three decades earlier in the shaping of our nation's destiny. The trip Lewis and Clark made from near St. Louis, Missouri, to the Pacific Ocean was the determining factor both in the course our history would take and in the eventual shape of our geographical boundaries. More than the seafaring traders who penetrated the West Coast ports, Lewis' and Clark's epic journey whetted America's appetite to extend the national boundaries from ocean to ocean. Those men who followed to trap and later to build houses and to plow the virgin soil were simply that — followers.

America in the early years of the nineteenth century consisted only of the land east of the Mississippi River. France and Spain alternately controlled the land west of the river to the Rocky Mountains, and Spain and England felt they controlled the remainder of the continent from the Continental Divide to the Pacific. There were no firm boundaries, only overlapping claims subject more to squatters' rights than to legal possession.

Although our history books speak of Manifest Destiny and other high-flown phrases, the simple fact is that various leaders in the United States, particularly Thomas Jefferson, wanted everything from the Atlantic to the Pacific. One way to get it, Jefferson believed, was to send out an exploring party to find out what was there and then bring back a report that would fire the imagination — or even greed — of the government and people so that they would want it, too.

Jefferson had long been interested in the West and had tried to launch other expeditions. In 1783, while serving in the Continental Congress, he wrote to General George Rogers Clark, asking him to lead an expedition into the West. Jefferson made this move after learning that Great Britain not only was planning a similar expedition but also already had money subscribed for it. In that same year a treaty was concluded in Paris granting the upper Ohio Valley — the Old Northwest — to the United States. General Clark was credited with saving that territory from foreign domination by defeating, during the Revolutionary War, the British forces under Lieutenant Governor Sir Henry Hamilton. General Clark's stock was very high then, but he was in financial troubles and had to turn down the offer. Also, the British expedition failed to materialize.

Two years later Jefferson, serving in Paris as the Confederation's minister to France, met an adventurer named John Ledyard, who has since been described accurately as part genius and part stargazer. Ledyard had a plan that was astonishing for the day, yet appealing to Jefferson: he wanted to cross the North American continent on foot. Actually, his credentials were excellent. He had sailed with Captain James Cook on his third and (for Captain Cook) fatal voyage that took them around the world, and Ledyard wrote a widely read book about the expedition in which he pointed out the possibility of fur trade in the American West.

Jefferson was intrigued by Ledyard's plan but was unable to raise funds for him or even arrange for a passage by ship to the northwest coast of America. Instead, Jefferson suggested that Ledyard take the long overland route: across Europe, Russia, and Siberia and then across the Pacific to Alaska in a Russian fur-trading boat. Ledyard liked the plan and in 1786, virtually penniless and without a passport, left with two dogs for companionship east across Europe.

He was one of the first international hitchhikers as he roamed eastward through Hamburg, Copenhagen, Finland, and into St. Petersburg (now Leningrad). He remained there from March to June, 1787 and finally left after a German scientist named Peter Simon Pallas of the Russian Academy of Sciences obtained a passport for him. Ledyard traveled all summer through Russia and arrived in the eastern Siberia town of Yakutsk in September. Winter prevented him from going farther and he holed up until February, 1788, when Russian officials arrested him, gave him a speedy trip back across Russia, and then deported him to Poland.

Why they arrested him is uncertain. Some researchers believe they distrusted his so-called scientific intentions; others believe he left St. Petersburg without the proper papers and permissions. Whatever the reason, another Jefferson plan failed and poor Ledyard died a year later in Cairo, Egypt, while on an expedition at the wrong end of Africa in search of the Niger River.

Jefferson didn't give up, although it would be fifteen years before his plan worked. He returned to the United States as Secretary of State and talked the American Philosophical Society in Philadelphia into raising funds to send a French botanist named André Michaux on a scientific journey to the Pacific. However, this trip failed because Michaux was a secret French agent, and the journey was called off when Michaux reached Louisville, Kentucky.

Interestingly, Michaux called on General Clark, whose younger brother, William, was living with him, attempting to put the general's affairs in order. General Clark's fortunes had taken a definite turn for the worse after several business ventures failed. A few years later, General Clark accepted a commission as general in the French army to lead an expedition against Louisiana and refused to surrender the commission when war between the United States and France seemed imminent. He took refuge in St. Louis.

During this time the only parts of the West familiar to the white man was the Pacific Coast and a small portion of the Missouri River. The Spanish and French had gone upriver as far as the Mandan villages near present-day Bismarck, North Dakota, and the British had worked downward from Canada to the same general area through the auspices of the North-West Fur Company and Hudson's Bay Company. But the vast plains to the west and the Rocky Mountains were still *terra incognita*.

Still another factor in this nagging interest in the West was the fabled Northwest Passage across the continent that would offer a shortcut to both the Pacific and Orient. At best, Jefferson and other supporters of the Lewis and Clark trip hoped the headwaters of the Missouri would be near an easily accessible pass which would involve only a short portage to the navigable headwaters of the Columbia River, thus making commerce by water practical. What they did not realize, of course, was the presence of the Bitterroot Range between the Rockies and the Snake River drainage, plus the tortuous streams that led to the Snake, and finally the Snake itself that was virtually impossible to navigate above its confluence with the Clearwater at the twin cities of Lewiston, Idaho, and Clarkston, Washington. It would be another century before the Northwest Passage was traversed and when Roald Amundsen did so in 1903–06, it was a route so impractical that it might as well not have existed.

One of Jefferson's first actions on becoming President in 1802 was to make an overture to the Spanish, who administered the Louisiana Territory although they had ceded it to France. He told the Spanish ambassador, Don Carlos Martinez, Marques de Casa Yrujo, of his intended exploration and tried to pass it off lightly as being of "literary" interest, which meant a purely scientific purpose. The Spaniard didn't believe him. He told his superiors that Jefferson was lying.

But Jefferson went ahead with plans for the expedition and appointed his personal secretary, Meriwether Lewis, its leader. Little is known of Lewis' exact secretarial duties, but it is generally accepted that Jefferson spent a great deal of time in tutoring Lewis in the natural sciences and in general preparing him for the mission.

Lewis told Jefferson he thought he could lead the expedition to the Pacific and back for an expenditure of about $2,500. This estimate turned out to be rather low, and the expedition was one of the new nation's first examples of cost overruns. The exact cost was subject to a number of variables, such as whether or not to include the soldiers' pay in the total since they would have been paid anyway. But the most often quoted figure is $38,722.25, still not a bad investment considering the results.

Jefferson had little trouble in obtaining congressional approval for the expedition and he released Lewis from his normal duties to begin preparations for it. Immediately Lewis wrote to his good friend, William Clark, offering him the position of

17

co-commander. They had served together under General "Mad Anthony" Wayne in the short-lived Whiskey Rebellion in Pennsylvania, the nation's first tax revolt. Both men had fought in Indian battles on the frontier, but most important, they were good friends and had respect for each other's ability.

To protect himself, Lewis also contacted another friend, Lieutenant Moses Hooke, a twenty-six-year-old officer in his old regiment, to go as co-commander should Clark be unable or unwilling. But Clark desperately wanted to go, and thus we have the Lewis and Clark rather than the Lewis and Hooke Expedition as part of our national heritage.

Although the fact is frequently overlooked, the expedition was actually a transcontinental voyage: Lewis was on the East Coast when he started and descended the Ohio River to the Mississippi to begin the voyage, which makes him the first white man to cross the country.

Lewis spent the spring and summer of 1803 preparing for the trip. He had to consult scientists to learn the rudiments of taxidermy, navigation and celestial observation, medicine, and Indian ethnology and history, and he had to purchase provisions and equipment. A partial list of his purchases include a quadrant, mariner's compass, pocket telescope, sextant, chronometer, magnet, and pole chains for surveying. He bought 193 pounds of "portable" soup in thirty-two containers (the men hated it), tents and camping equipment, clothing and blankets, medicines and surgical instruments, many rifles, pistols, and the small cannons to mount on his boats, tools, and items to trade.

The last-mentioned is one of the more interesting on his shopping list. It included 4,600 assorted needles, 2,800 assorted fishhooks, 1,152 moccasin awls, 500 brooches, 180 scissors, 180 pewter looking glasses, 130 pigtails of tobacco, 122 handkerchiefs, 73 bundles of assorted beads, 72 pieces of striped ribbon, 48 calico ruffled shirts, 12 pipe tomahawks, 11½ pounds of beads, and 1 quart of vermilion.

The air gun which surprised Indians along the route because it was both silent and accurate

Even this was not enough. During the winter of 1804-05 in Mandan they were so low on some items that the expedition's blacksmiths were kept busy forging gifts and items so that they could barter for food to sustain them through the remainder of the journey.

A few days before Lewis left Washington on his journey, Jefferson told him that negotiations had been completed for the purchase of the Louisiana Territory —more than 820,000 square miles for about $15 million, a better deal even than the Manhattan Island purchase. The French had overextended themselves in the New World and were in financial straits at home and happy to make the sale.

Yet the Spanish were concerned about the expedition and through a series of double dealings and opportunistic ploys, they actually launched three missions from Santa Fe against "Captain Merry" to intercept the explorers. At one time the Spanish forces came within 100 miles of Lewis' and Clark's route, but the expeditions were poorly organized and they were unsuccessful in cutting Lewis and Clark off and forcing them to return.

Lewis first went to Pittsburgh, Pennsylvania, to oversee construction of a keelboat, but he was forced to remain there and agonize over the delay because the boatbuilder was both a drunkard and a laggard. Lewis had hoped to start the upriver expedition in late summer, 1803 and spend the winter somewhere on the river far from civilization. But the continual delays led to his reluctant decision to winter at St. Louis. It was probably just as well that he was delayed, considering his problems with the members of the Corps of Discovery.

But all news was not bad at Pittsburgh. Lewis received a letter from Clark saying he would be delighted to serve as co-commander, although their ranks were different. Lewis generously insisted that Clark refer to himself as a captain, too, although the promised promotion did not come due to a top-heavy peacetime army.

So frustrated did Lewis become in Pittsburgh over the slowness of the boatbuilding that he considered scrapping the keelboat plan and setting off for St. Louis in two pirogues, flat-bottomed dugouts common on the frontier rivers. But he was talked out of that idea because it was so impractical, considering the amount of goods he had to transport down the Ohio. Instead, he sat and fumed until the keelboat was ready. It was

The keelboat which went from the Ohio River to Mandan and back to St. Louis

fifty-five feet long and slightly over eight feet wide amidships. It carried a thirty-two foot mast with a jointed base so that it could be lowered and had a large square main sail along with a smaller foresail. The forecastle deck was ten feet long and the stern had a cabin beneath an elevated deck.

He and some recruits, probably including George Shannon, the youngest member of the crew, set off for St. Louis with Scannon, a black Newfoundland dog Lewis bought for twenty dollars and took to the Pacific and back. They had a rough time on the Ohio River because it was running low in the late summer, and they often had to hire teams of horses to haul the keelboat over shallows. They could cover an average distance of only twelve miles a day downstream, with much time spent unloading the keelboat to lighten the load, then reloading until the next shallows.

By the time Lewis reached Cincinnati he was reduced to two recruits for the trip, having dismissed the others for reasons he did not specify in correspondence. In addition to the seventeen or eighteen-year-old George Shannon, he had now signed on John Colter. Colter left the family farm near Staunton, Virginia to intercept Lewis at a place called Old Limestone, near present-day Maysville, Kentucky. Colter became one of the expedition's most resourceful and famous graduates by discovering what is now Yellowstone National Park, nicknamed "Colter's Hell" until others saw it and believed it. He also gained fame for his exploits in escaping from a band of Blackfeet Indians who stripped him naked, gave him a head start, and tried to run him down. Colter by then was a man of considerable experience and was never a fool. Rather than try to outrun the Indians, he hid in a beaver lodge until they gave up the hunt, then crawled out of the river and strolled stark naked to the nearest fort 200 miles away.

Scannon, Lewis' dog

Probably the first scientific task undertaken by Lewis on his assignment was a stop at Big Bone Lick, Kentucky where he acquired some mammoth bones and sent them back to Jefferson, together with a detailed report, something of a rehearsal for the coming years.

But Lewis, always susceptible to the impatient course, was upset by the delays and disappointed that he would have to winter so close to civilization. He wanted to get on with it. So he wrote to Jefferson that he would spend part of the coming winter on a side expedition, a solo horseback journey on the south side of the Missouri River, possibly as far south as Santa Fe. Jefferson put an immediate stop to the plan and told Lewis in a letter dated November 16, 1804 that "The object of your mission is single; the direct water communication from sea to sea formed by the bed of the Missouri & perhaps the Oregon." So much for that.

When Lewis and his crew finally reached the Falls of the Ohio at the twin cities of Louisville, Kentucky, and Clarksville, Indiana Territory, the man who was to be his constant companion during the expedition was waiting for him. William Clark, at thirty-three, was four years older than Lewis, stood six feet tall, and was described as having a strong physique. He was outgoing, almost always cheerful, resourceful, and of even temperament. In many ways he was the opposite of his friend, Lewis, who tended to be moody and introspective and was sometimes given to melancholia. They always got along well and if they quarreled or violently disagreed during the long journey, no record of the event exists. It was the rare case of two men of different temperaments complementing each other, balancing each other's shortcomings. It is worth noting that Lewis and Clark scholars have found very little to complain about in Clark's behavior, and the only mistakes in judgment were those made by Lewis. Surely Clark made errors during the expedition —no one is perfect—but they were not recorded, nor were they apparently as serious as Lewis' episode among the Blackfeet Indians on the return journey.

After nearly two weeks in Clarksville, the party left on October 26, 1803, to complete the first leg of the mission. By that time they had accumulated nineteen members: the two leaders; Clark's servant (a tidy euphemism for slave), York; nine permanent members, and seven soldiers on temporary assignment to them. And of course the big dog, Scannon. When they arrived at Fort Massac, near present-day Metropolis, Illinois, they signed on the best member of the entire party, George Drouillard (the famous Drewyer of the journals), who apparently was a civilian employee at the fort. Drouillard was an excellent woodsman, an expert marksman, a good companion, skilled interpreter (it is believed he was half-Shawnee), a sharp-eyed scout, and as tough as he was reliable. The captains soon came to depend on him above all others and there is no record of Drouillard's disappointing them.

After picking up two more men at Fort Massac, they continued down the Ohio to the Mississippi, then poled and towed up it to establish a winter camp at Wood River, Illinois, after investigating other sites along the way. They chose the eastern bank of the Mississippi because it was in the United States, whereas the land across the river was still in the disputed Louisiana Territory.

Soon after a shack city had been erected, it became apparent that Lewis' plan to leave immediately was not a sound one. He and Clark spent a great deal of time whipping the men (literally and figuratively) into shape as an expeditionary force. Discipline was a continual problem and court-martial records flourished during the winter. The leaders held frequent shooting matches and constantly tried to impress upon the men the importance of doing the job they had signed on for. It was a long winter with considerable boredom, relieved occasionally by whiskey traders who set up camp nearby, and the inevitable brawls that erupt when young, tough men are confined too long.

Lewis and Clark were involved with governmental affairs in St. Louis, including representing Jefferson in ceremonies transferring the Louisiana Territory to the United States. They were also busy purchasing more gear to outfit the party and increasing the size of their complement from the ten or twelve they had originally planned. The smaller number was simply impractical for so ambitious an undertaking. More men were needed both for numerical safety and to propel the boats up the evil Missouri River.

Reuben Gold Thwaites, the earliest and perhaps foremost Lewis and Clark scholar, gives this generally accepted list of members, as verified against the official payroll at the expedition's end:

Meriwether Lewis, Captain in the 1st Regt., Infantry; William Clark, 2nd Lieutenant in the Artillery; Sergeants Charles Floyd, Patrick Gass, John Ordway, and Nathaniel Pryor; Privates William Bratton, John Colter, John Collins, Pierre Cruzatte, Joseph Field, Reuben Field, Robert Frazier, George Gibson, Silas Goodrich, Hugh Hall, Thomas P. Howard, Francis Labiche, Hugh McNeal, John Potts, George Shannon, John Shields, John B. Thompson, William Werner, Joseph Whitehouse, Alexander Willard, Richard Windsor, Peter Wiser, and York.

In addition there were two interpreters, George Drouillard and Toussaint Charbonneau, and the young Indian woman, Sacajawea ("Bird Woman"), Charbonneau's wife. The last two were added at Fort Mandan.

Two soldiers, John Newman and M. B. Reed, who started with the expedition, were written out of the journals by being court-martialed for misconduct and sent back to St. Louis on April 7, 1805, after wintering with the party at Fort Mandan. Baptiste Lepage was enlisted in Newman's place at Fort Mandan on November 2, 1804 and remained with the party until the end.

Yet another, who did not appear on the payroll, was Sacajawea's son born at Fort Mandan. However, he was rewarded by having a striking geographical feature, Pompeys Pillar in Montana, named after him, and later Clark arranged for his education.

The journals proper began that winter at Wood River, and scholars must rely on letters and government records to piece together earlier events. One of the first entries in the official journals by Clark describing the area around Wood River gives an immediate suggestion of the acute power of observation the leaders possessed and the inconsistent spelling that for decades has amused and sometimes irritated their readers.

"The Country about the Mouth of Missouri is pleasent rich and partially Settled On the East Side of the Mississippi a leavel rich bottom extends back about 3 miles, and rises by several elevations to the high Country which is thinly timbered with Oakes & On the lower Side of the Missouri, at about 2 miles back the Country rises graduilly, to a high plesent thinly timbered Country, the lands are generally fine on the river bottoms and well calculating for farming on the upper Country.

"in the point of the Bottom is extensive and emensly rich for 15 or 20 miles up each river, and about 2/3 of which is open leavel plains in which the inhabtents of St. Charles & portage de Scioux had their crops of corn & wheat. On the upland is a fine farming country partially timbered for Some distance back."

And one of Lewis' early entries is a record of his vexation at the men, one in particular. His detachment order for March 3, 1804, shows an effort to reason with them. However, the order-essay is so long that few probably listened all the way through as Sgt. Ordway read it to them:

"The Commanding officer feels himself mortifyed and disappointed at the disorderly conduct of Reubin Fields, in refusing to mount guard when in the dur roteen of duty he was regularly warned; nor is he less surprised at the want of discretion in those who urged his opposition to the faithfull discharge of his duty, particularly, [John] Shields, whose sense of propryety he had every reason to believe would have induced him reather to have promoted good order, than to have excited disorder and faction among the party, particularly in the absence of Capt Clark and himself; The Commanding officer is also sorry to find any man, who has been engaged by himself and Capt Clark for the expedition on which they have entered, so destitute of understanding, as not to be able to draw the distinction between being placed under the command of another officer, whose will in such case would be their law, and that of obeying the orders of Capt Clark and himself communicated to them through Sergt. Ordway, who, as one of the party, has during their necessary absence been charged with the execution of their orders; action from those orders expressly, and not from his own caprice, and who, in all respect accountable to us for the faithfull observance of the same.

"A moments reflection must convince every man of our party, that were we to neglect the more important and necessary arrangements in relation to the voyage we are now entering on, for the purpose of remaining at camp in order to communicate our orders in person to the individuals of the party. . . ."

The order continues. One can imagine the men nodding off and snapping awake sharply while Sgt. Ordway, under orders, read the document to them.

While history has seemed to have gone out of its way to obscure most members of the party, some information about them has been unearthed. They came from most of the original thirteen colonies and one, John Potts, was born in Germany. Most were young men. Some were illiterate, others barely literate, whereas Ordway and Shannon apparently were well educated by contemporary standards. Some of the men had no experience whatsoever in the wilderness, but most of them did, and they also had other practical skills; Shields was a good blacksmith, gunsmith, and general fix-it man.

It was a long winter. Clark was ill much of the time with bronchial problems, a common malady in the cold, humid St. Louis area, and the men were relegated to various menial tasks that in some instances most surely were in the make-work category loved so dearly by the military mind. There were also useful tasks, such as modifying the keelboat to make it more adaptable to their purposes. Additional lockers were installed with lids that would double as a breastwork in the event of an Indian attack. They added ridgepoles over the boat to support awnings against the sun and storms and installed small swivel cannons, a heavy one on the bow and two smaller ones on the stern, plus other small ones on the two pirogues.

They had all the provisions, spare parts, ammunition, trade goods, and scientific instruments to pack and repack. They divided up the material so that if one boat were lost, they wouldn't be stranded without necessities. They also repacked the trade goods and gifts for Indians along the way into fourteen bales and one box so that when they opened them one at a time, everything would be there. Also, one suspects, they did not care for the Indians knowing there were that many individual packages.

Just before they left, an incident occurred that proved the friendship of the leaders and bespoke Lewis' character. It was understood that Clark would receive a promotion to captain so that their command would be equal in rank as well as in their private understanding. However, Clark's expected promotion in the Corps of Engineers was turned down by the War Department because there were no vacancies in a peacetime army. Instead, he received only a commission as 2nd lieutenant in the Corps of Artillerists. But Lewis insisted they keep Clark's actual rank secret from the rest of the men and carry on accordingly as co-commanders, which they did.

They finally began loading the keel boat on May 7, 1804 and took it out onto the Mississippi for a trial run to test its balance and handling characteristics, then brought it back to adjust the load. Three days later Clark issued every man 100 balls for their rifles and two pounds of buckshot for their muskets. The next day, May 11, Drouillard brought the group of seven French boatmen in from St. Louis to help them as far as the Mandan villages, then to return to St. Louis with the keelboat and the reports and specimens the explorers would collect along the route. On the morning of May 14, they departed, and Clark wrote:

"Rained the fore part of the day I determined to go as far as St. Charles a french Village 7 leag. up the Missourie, and wait at that place untill Capt. Lewis could finish the business in which he was obliged to attend to at St. Louis and join me by Land from that place 24 miles; by this movement I calculated that if any alterations in the loading of the Vestles or other changes necessary, that they might be made at St. Charles.

"I set out at 4 o'clock P.M., in the presence of many of the neighboring inhabitents, and proceeded on under a jentle brease up the Missourie to the upper Point of the 1st Island 4 Miles and camped on the Island which is Situated Close on the right (or Starboard) Side, and opposit the mouth of a Small Creek called Cold Water, a heavy rain this after-noon."

Thus the adventure began.

2

*St. Louis
to Mandan*

The departure from Wood River constituted both the beginning of the journey and a shakedown cruise because Lewis and some of the men were still in St. Louis making final preparations. Clark wrote: "I determined to go as far as St. Charles a french village 7 leags. up the Missourie. and wait at that place until Capt. Lewis could finish the business in which he was obliged to attend to at St. Louis and join me by land from that place 24 miles; By this movement I calculated that if any alterations in the loading of the Vestles or other Changes necessary, that they might be made at St. Charles.''

Across the broad river they went in three boats: a keelboat fifty-five feet long with one large square sail and twenty-two oars, and two pirogues with six and seven oars, one painted white and the other red.

It took the party two days to row and sail to St. Charles, then a town of some 100 shacks along the riverfront with about 450 residents. They stayed there five days, completing the loading and taking on more personnel, including the multilingual half-Indian Pierre Cruzatte and Francis Labiche who signed on as boatmen but who were often used as interpreters.

Discipline continued to be a problem as the crewmen celebrated with a bit too much enthusiasm, including the trouble-maker, John Collins, who was court-martialed for being AWOL, misbehaving at a ball given by townspeople, and using disrespectful language to Clark. For his sins he was given fifty lashes. William Werner and Hugh Hall were also punished for being AWOL but receive only twenty-five lashes. (Apparently they didn't talk back to Lewis or Clark.)

Finally, at 3:30 P.M., May 21, the Corps of Discovery departed St. Charles for the upriver journey that would keep them away for more than two years. The last village they passed was La Charette, a cluster of seven cottages on the riverbank that had been founded sometime in the 1760s near present-day Marthasville and has long since been covered by the shifting river's course.

Along this portion of the Missouri they met eight parties of traders returning behind the spring breakup to St. Louis. From them they obtained recent information on the river conditions and the upriver Indians. Often they traded items and in one case recruited another member, Pierre Dorian (''Old Dorian''), who had lived for twenty years among the Sioux. They hired him primarily to help convince some of the Sioux chiefs that they should go to Washington to meet with President Jefferson.

After a few days on the river, the crew settled into a routine that was to continue all the way to Mandan that year. They traveled from four or five to twenty-six or twenty-seven miles a

Mosquitoes *(left)* and ticks *(right)*

day, depending on river conditions, weather, and general health. The river was especially treacherous in that stretch across the present state of Missouri, and the men were often in danger and the boats threatened to swamp innumerable times. The channel meandered from one season to another, sandbars grew and disappeared with regularity, and the bank was frequently undercut and caved into the river — once almost taking the men with it while they slept. The riverbed itself was strewn with uprooted trees. Called sawyers, these trees were anchored to the silty bottom, their branches swaying back and forth, often lurking just beneath the murky surface. At other times they would break loose and knock men off their feet, strike the boats or snag them, forcing the crews to drift backward and go around them.

Everyone was plagued by mosquitoes, flies, ticks, chiggers, the hot sun, and sudden, vicious thunderstorms that whipped the sail and threatened to swamp them. Men spent virtually entire days up to their waists in the swift river, pulling the boats along, going for days without ever being completely dry.

29

While one crew manned the boats, other groups foraged along the riverbanks during the day, searching for game to feed the crew. Usually Lewis, the better trained naturalist of the two, stayed on shore walking or riding one of the horses in search of new species of plants and animals to report to and collect for President Jefferson. Clark, a more congenial sort and more experienced on the water, preferred to stay with the boats and the men, and this is the way they usually traveled. At each day's end they filled their journals with detailed descriptions of the daily events and recorded topography, drainage, plant and wildlife, mineral resources, distances and directions, meteorological data, mapping, and other scientific information.

Captain Lewis was trained — after a fashion — in medicine, and he spent a great deal of time treating injuries and ailments among the forty-six men with them on this stretch of the trip. His journal entries mention boils, abscesses, sore feet, sunstroke, dysentery, fever, snakebites, headaches, colic, and rheumatism. One of the most popular forms of treatment — something of a cure that can kill — was draining blood from the patient; judging from the number of references in the journals to this rather barbaric treatment, enough blood must have been drained to stock a blood bank for a small city.

American raven *(Corvus corax sinuatus)*   Western common crow *(Corvus brachyrhynchos hesperis)*

Plains horned toad *(Phrynosoma cornutum)*

The first major geographical division was reached on June 26, when they swung nearly due north at present-day Kansas City, Missouri. Here they set up camp for a few days near two Kansas Indian villages that were vacant while the residents presumably were hunting buffalo out on the plains to the west. They took a break to repair the equipment and to let the men rest and nurse their sore feet and bodies, then went on northward to present Atchison, Kansas, where they celebrated July 4, 1804, with cannon fire and an extra issue of whiskey.

During this westward journey the captains were busy collecting specimens and noting various species seen along the way. They found an eastern wood rat (*Neotoma floridana*), a plains horned toad (*Phrynosoma cornutum*), and Osage orange (*Toxylon pomiferum*) and collected some of the latter to send back to President Jefferson the following spring.

They reached the Platte River on July 21, sixty-nine days out of Camp Wood, in the heart of Pawnee and Oto Indian country. A group of eight men, including Lewis and Clark, walked up the Platte a short distance looking for the Indians so they could hold a council. They had seen no Indians since leaving St. Charles and were anxious to carry out Jefferson's orders regarding councils along the route. In spite of ample evidence of Indians, they didn't see any until Drouillard found a Missouri Indian while out hunting and brought him back to the river. The Indian explained that he lived in a camp of Otos of about twenty lodges away from the river and that the rest of the small band was out hunting buffalo. They sent one of the boatmen, Joseph Barter La Liberte, with the Indian to the camp to invite the Otos to a council, then struck out upriver again and stopped after about fifty miles at a place they called "Councile Bluff or Handsom Prarie," the site of present-day Council Bluffs, Iowa.

Osage orange (*Maclura aurantiaca*)

Two days later, on August 2, a group of Otos and Missouris arrived with a trader whom the explorers called Mr. Fairfong.

31

Western badger *(Taxidea taxus neglecta)*

But La Liberte was not with them. In the group were six chiefs of a minor category and when Lewis and Clark learned there were about 250 Indians in the area, the entire detachment was placed on battle station alert for safety's sake. The next morning the council began under the awning formed by the keelboat's sail. The soldiers performed a parade for the chiefs and had all their weaponry showing in order to impress on the Indians that there would be no foolishness. Then one of the captains delivered a long speech through an interpreter which explained the incomprehensible to the Indians: that the government of the territory had gone from Spain to France to the United States. The Indians probably thought this was nice for the explorers to talk about, but it surely sounded a bit foreign since it was their land under question. The captains also described how the new Great White Father wanted to become acquainted with the Indians (his "children") and emphasized the need for peace both among the tribes and toward the whites.

Then the Indians got their turn at speechmaking; they said they would take everything into consideration and then passed the peace pipe around. Lewis and Clark distributed gifts that included medals struck especially for the expedition, flags, clothing, ammunition, and whiskey.

Nearly all councils held along the route followed this general format, and a major part of the success of the expedition was the spirit of respect and firmness shown by the explorers.

The council ended the next day, La Liberte still missing, but the explorers headed upriver without him. Then M. B. Reed, one of the privates, said he had forgotten his knife at the last camp and asked permission to go back for it. It was granted and when he didn't return, it became apparent he had deserted, as had La Liberte. When neither had returned by August 7, Lewis and Clark dispatched the indispensible Drouillard, together with Reuben Field, William Bratton, and Francis Labiche to go back after them. Drouillard was told to kill Reed, if necessary.

They didn't return until August 18, but when they did, they had Reed with them. La Liberte had escaped again and they let him go since he was a civilian. But Reed stood court-martial and was found guilty. His punishment was to run the gauntlet four times while the men flogged his bare back. The Otos who accompanied the Drouillard party back were appalled by the punishment. Reed also was dishonorably discharged and assigned to menial chores until he could return with the keelboat the following spring to St. Louis.

It was Lewis' birthday and the crew put aside the whips and sticks they'd used on Reed and were issued an extra gill (one-fourth pint) of whiskey.

During the night, however, Sergeant Floyd became seriously ill and was unable to eat. The captains diagnosed his illness as colic, but doctors today believe it was peritonitis from a ruptured appendix. He had been very ill about three weeks earlier but had seemed to recover. This time the inflammation was fatal. In spite of all their medical lore, Floyd died aboard a boat the next morning just before noon. They landed at what is now Sioux City, Iowa, and carried his body to the top of the highest hill in the area for burial. They marked the spot with a post with Floyd's name and date of death on it. Two days later the men selected Patrick Gass, the carpenter as Floyd's replacement.

Floyd was the first American soldier to die west of the Mississippi and the only casualty of the entire Lewis and Clark expedition, and even if a trained surgeon had been along, the odds are he still would have died; the first successful appendectomy wasn't performed until 1887.

As a footnote to the site of Floyd's grave, the cedar post the explorers erected on the hill was something of a beacon for river travelers over a number of decades, but the river swung to the east during the 1850s. In 1857 a spring flood carved away a portion of the hill, and bones — apparently those of Floyd — were seen protruding from the eroded bluff. Sioux City residents decided to save them and lowered a man by rope over the cliff edge for them. In May, 1857, ceremonies were held to bury the bones again at their present location. However, no marker was placed and the exact location was lost until 1895 when the *Sioux City Journal* began a campaign to rediscover the grave.

A group of people present at the 1857 internment picked the most likely spot and the digging began again. They found the coffin and some bones. A Floyd's Memorial Association was formed and money collected, and on the ninety-first anniversary of his death, August 20, 1895, his bones were removed from the casket, placed in an urn, and reburied. In May, 1899, the association purchased twenty-two acres around the gravesite and raised $20,000 in federal, state, and private funds for the monument that stands there today, a 100-foot obelisk of yellow sandstone, clearly visible from the river and the highway from both north and south ends of town. It is surrounded by an iron fence and illuminated at night.

The river changes direction again near Sioux City and swings to the northwest, and it is here that the Great Plains begin making inroads into the dense timber of the Midwest. The explorers began noticing more and more open country with copses of trees in low spots.

They were still plagued by mosquitoes in the flat country and complained that even using a branch to wave like a fan didn't keep them away. They only avoided them with another natural malady, the frequent thunderstorms that sweep the Midwest and Great Plains throughout the summer. A gentle breeze is usually sufficient to keep the mosquitoes from launching attacks on warm-blooded creatures.

As usual, the captains kept meticulous notes and their journals of each day's activities are remarkable for the good cheer under trying conditions, the details, and the occasional wit.

On August 27 they made their first contact with the Sioux Indians when they met three of them near the mouth of the James River. Clark sent Sgt. Pryor and Old Dorian with a French boatman up the James to invite the chiefs to a council. They appeared the following day and the camp was made on the Nebraska side of the river at the foot of Calumet Bluff near where the Gavins Point Dam was built across the river from Yankton, South Dakota. With the chiefs were about seventy men and boys and the council was held beneath a large oak tree. Clark noted that the Indians "brought with them for their own use 2 Elk & 6 deer which the young men Killed on the way from their Camp 12 Miles distant.

"Sergt. Pryor informs me that When (they) came near the Indian Camp they were met by men with a Buffalow roabe to carry them, Mr. Dorian informed me they were not the owners of the Boats & did not wish to be carried the Scioues Camps are handsom of a Conic form Covered with Buffalow Roabs Painted different colours and all compact & handsomly arranged, Covered all round an open part in the Centre for the fire, with Buffalow roabs, each Lodg has a place for Cooking detached, the lodges contain from 10 to 15 persons. a Fat Dog was presented as a mark of their Great respect for the party of which they partook hartily and thought it good and well flavored."

The following morning Clark noted "a verry thick fog" and told how they sent Dorian across the river in a pirogue for the chiefs and warriors to hold council under an oak tree where the men had a flag flying on a tall flagstaff. Lewis delivered the speech this time and gave a medal, some clothes, trade goods, and some tobacco. The grand chief received a flag and certificate (which were given as proof that each main chief represented his tribe), a hat, and artillery coat, the latter two items both richly decorated with lace.

The only sour note came from Dorian, who complained bitterly that Lewis and Clark did not invite him to eat with the leaders. Clark said Dorian apologized later, however.

Dorian's trip with the explorers ended here. The captains wanted to take some chiefs back to Washington with them when the journey ended and since the Sioux were so peaceful and the council had gone so well, they decided to sell the Yankton Sioux on the idea. Dorian was talked into staying with them over the next two winters both to help to negotiate peace between them and other Indians and to organize a contingent to visit the President. He was successful, but the episode had tragic consequences for some members of the Corps.

Four days earlier Drouillard and young Shannon had been left behind to look for lost horses, but the following day Drouillard showed up with neither the horses nor Shannon. Joseph Field and John Shields were sent back to hunt for Shannon and the horses "with derections to keep on the Hills to the Grand Calumet above on River Kacure (the Niobrara)." Two days later they returned with the news that Shannon and the horses were ahead of the party and they could not overtake him. "This man not being a first-rate Hunter, we deturmined to Send one man in pursute of him with some Provisions," Clark wrote.

Pelicans *(Pelecanus erythrorhynchus)*

In the meantime the council with the Sioux was held and the explorers worked with the Indians, recording their vocabulary, which they did all the way across the country, none of which survived. They continued the upriver trip, taking game almost at will from the dense herds that roamed the plains and came down to the river to drink. On September 10, for example, they killed three buffalo and one elk, and the next day Clark killed an elk, two deer, and some squirrels, and the men killed another elk, two deer, and a pelican. No one had to go hungry, and they assumed that young Shannon, wherever he was, had enough to eat even though he was not an expert marksman. But they were wrong. He was found on September 16, and Clark was astonished at the situation:

"here the Man who left us with the horses 22 [actually only sixteen] days ago, *George Shannon He started 26 Aug.* and has been a head ever since joined us nearly Starved to Death, he had been 12 days without anything to eate but Grapes & one Rabit, which he Killed by shooting a piece of hard Stick in place of a ball. This Man Supposeing the boat to be a head pushed on as long as he could, when he became weak and feable deturmined to lay by and waite for a tradeing boat, which is expected, Keeping one horse for the last resorse, thus a man had like to have Starved to death in a land of Plenty for the want of Bullits or Something to kill his meat. we Camped on the L.S. above the mouth of a run . . ." Clearly the seventeen-or eighteen-year-old Shannon had a lot to learn.

By this time the explorers were out of the wooded hills and into the High Plains country of the Dakotas. Lewis, who either had not been keeping a journal or lost it, resumed note taking and displayed his acute powers of observation and description in the entry for Monday, September 17, 1804: "Having for many days past confined myself to the boat, I determined to devote this day to amuse myself on shore with my gun and view the interior of the country lying between the river and the Corvus Creek (now Crow Creek). accordingly before sunrise I set out with six of my best hunters, two of whom I dispatched to the lower side of Corvus Creek, two with orders to hunt the bottums and woodland on the river, while I retained two others to accompany me in the intermediate country. one quarter of a mile in rear of our camp which was situated in a fine open grove of cotton wood passed a grove of plumb trees loaded with fruit and now ripe, observed but little difference betwen this fruit and that of a similar kind common to the Atlantic States. the trees are smaller and more thickly set. this forrest of plumb trees garnish a plain about 20 feet more elivated than that on which we

Black-tailed prairie dogs *(Cynomys ludovicianus ludovicianus)*

37

Coyote *(Canis latrans latrans)*

were encamped; this plain extends back about a mile to the foot of the hills one mile distant and to which it is gradually ascending   this plane extends with the same bredth from the creek below to the distance of near three miles above parrallel with the river, and its is intirely occupyed by the burrows of the *barking squiril* [prairie dog] hertefore described; this anamal appears here in infinite numbers   and the shortness and virdu[r]e of grass gave the plain the appearance throughout it's whole extent of beautifull bowling-green in fine order . . . a great number of wolves of the small kind [probably coyote], halks [hawks] and some pole-cats were to be seen. I presume that those anamals feed on this squirril. found the country in every direction for about three miles intersected with deep revenes and steep irregular hills of 100 to 200 feet high; at the tops of these hills the country breakes of as usual into a fine leavel plain extending as far as the eye can reach. from this plane I had an extensive view of the river below, and the irregular hills which border the opposite sides of the river and creek. the surrounding country had been birnt about a month before and young grass had now sprung up to hight of 4 Inches presenting the live green of the spring to the West a high range of

Bald eagle *(Haliaeetus leucocephalus)*

hills, strech across the country from N. to S. and appeared
distant about 20 miles; they are not very extensive as I could
plainly observe their rise and termination   no rock appeared on
them and the sides were covered with virdu[r]e similar to that of
the plains   this senery already rich pleasing and beautiful was
still farther hightened by immence herds of Buffaloe, deer Elk
and Antelopes which we saw in every direction feeding on the
hills and plains. I do not think I exagerate when I estimate the
number of Buffaloe which could be compre [hend]ed at one
view to amount to 3000. my object if possible to kill a female
Antelope having already procured a male; I pursued my rout on
this plain to the west flanked by my two hunters untill eight in
the morning when I made the signal for them to come to me
which they did shortly after. we rested our selves about half an
hour, and regailed ourselves on half a bisquit each and some

Striped skunk
(*Mephitis mephitis
hudsonica*)

Buffalo *(Bison bison)*

Antelope

jirks of Elk which we had taken the precaution to put in our pouches in the morning before we set out, and drank of the water of a small pool which had collected on this plain from the rains which had fallen some days before. we had now after various windings in pursuit of several herds of antelopes which we had seen on our way made the distance of about eight miles from our camp. we found the Antelope extreemly shye and watchful insomuch that we had been unable to get a shot at them; when at rest they generally select the most elivated point in the neighborhood, and as they are watchful and extreemly quick of sight and their sense of smelling very accute it is almost impossible to approach them within gunshot; in short they will frequently discover and flee from you at the distance of three miles. I had this day an opportunity of witnessing the agility and the superior fleetness of this anamal which was to me really astonishing. I had pursued and twice suprised a small herd of seven, in the first instance they did not discover me distinctly and therefore did not run at full speed, tho' they took care before they rested to gain an elivated point where it was impossible to approach them under cover, except in one direction and that happened to be in the direction from which the wind blew towards them; bad as the chance to approach them was, I made the best of my way towards them, frequently peeping over the ridge with which I took care to conceal myself from their view the male, of which there was but one, frequently incircled the summit of the hill on which the females stood in a group, as if to look out for the approach of danger. I got within about 200 paces of them when they smelt me and fled; I gained the top of the eminence on which they stood, as soon as possible from whence I had an extensive view of the country the antilopes which had disappeared in a steep reveene now appeared at the distance of about three miles on the side of a ridge which passed obliquely across me and extended about four miles. so soon had these antelopes gained the distance at which they had again appeared to my view I doubted at ferst that they were the same that I had just surprised, but my doubts soon vanished when I beheld the rapidity of their flight along the ridge before me it appeared reather the rappid flight of birds than the motion of quadrupeds. I think I can safely venture the asscertion that the speed of this anamal is equal if not superior to that of the finest blooded courser.''

Although the trip through the plains was punctuated with idyllic moments such as this one, the party was constantly on the alert for the fearsome Teton Sioux, whose territory they were entering. This powerful tribe, one of the most aggressive on the Missouri River, had been steadily forcing other tribes westward and for decades had given the Spanish and French traders problems. They had been demanding that they receive firearms from the traders and that the traders not permit other tribes along the river to have them. They also demanded that they and they alone deal with the other tribes and that the white traders treat them as the middlemen. Lewis and Clark had heard all these stories during the previous winter in St. Louis, and their poor opinion of the Tetons was reinforced by meetings enroute with the traders and other Indians.

Yet the explorers were determined to show no fear of the tribe and stayed four days among them, even though Lewis called them "the vilest miscreants of the human race." Their first meeting was on September 23 when three boys swam the river to the camp and told them there were eighty lodges in one of their camps and sixty in the other not far ahead. Lewis and Clark gave the boys some tobacco for the chiefs and an invitation to a council. The following morning they set out and "prepared all thing for Action in Case of necessity, our Perogus went to the Island for the Meet, Soon after the man on Shore run up the bank and reported that the Indians had Stolen the horse We Soon after Met 5 Inds. and ankered out Som distance & Spoke to them informed them we were friends, & Wished to Continue So but were not afraid of any Indians, Some of their young men had taken the horse Sent by their Great father for their Cheif and we would not Speek to them untill the horse was returned to us again.''

They moved on upstream and anchored off the mouth of the Bad River (which they named the Teton) and began the tense wait.

Clark's entry in the journal for September 25 begins innocently enough, as most of their journal entries did, with the comment that it was "a fair Morning the wind from the S.E. all well,'' and so forth. But before the day was over, they had survived the first war of nerves of the trip. Clark tells the story succinctly:

"Envited those Cheifs on board to Show them our boat and such Curiossities as was Strange to them, we gave them ¼ of a glass of Whiskey which they appeared to be verry fond of, Sucked the bottle after it was out & Soon began to be troublesom, one of the 2nd Cheif assumeing Drunkness, as a Cloake for his rascally intentions I went with those Cheifs (in one of the Perogues with 5 men — 3 & 2 Ind.) (which left the boat with great reluctiance) to Shore with a view of reconsileing those men to us, as Soon as I landed the Perogue three of their young Men Seased the Cable of the Perogue, (in which we had pressents & etc.) the Chiefs Soldr [each chief had a soldier] Huged the mast, and the 2nd Chief was verry insolent both in words & jestures (pretended Drunkenness & staggered up against me) declareing I should not go on, Stateing he had not receved presents sufficient from us, his justures were of Such a personal nature I felt My self Compeled to Draw my Sword (and Made a Signal to the boat to prepare for action) at this Motion Capt. Lewis ordered all under arms in the boat, those with me also Showed a Disposition to Defend themselves and me, the grand Chief then took hold of the roap & ordered the young Warrers away, I felt My Self warm & Spoke in verry positive terms.

"Most of the Warriers appeared to have ther Bows strung and took out thier arrows from the quiver. as I (being surrounded) was not permitted (by them) to return, I Sent all the men except 2 Inps [interpreters] to the boat, the perogue Soon returned with about 12 of their determined men ready for any event. this movement caused a no: of the Indians to withdraw at a distance, (leaving their chiefs & soldiers alone with me). Their treatment to me was verry rough & I think justified roughness on my part, they all lift my Perogue, and Councild with themselves the result I could not lern and nearly all went off after remaining in this Situation Some time I offered my hand to the 1. & 2. Chiefs who refusd to receve it. I turned off & went with my men on board the perogue. I had not prosd more (than) 10 paces before the 1st Cheif 3rd & 2 Brave Men Waded in after me. I took them in & went on board.

"We proceeded on about 1 Mile & anchored out off a Willow Island placed a guard on Shore to protect the Cooks & a guard in the boat, fastened the Perogues to the boat, I call this Island bad humered Island as we were in a bad humer."

The next day was a bit milder, although it had its tense moments, too. The party started up river early in the morning but anchored again after the Indians pleaded with them to stay another night so they could show the white men their good intentions. Lewis and Clark agreed but did not relax their vigil against troublemakers.

Clark described them as being "Spritely," yet generally ill looking people with small arms and legs and given to blackening their faces with charcoal and grease. The squaws were "Chearfull fine look'g womin not handsom, do all their laborious work & I may Say perfect Slaves to the Men, as all Squars of Nations much at War, or where the Womin are more noumerous than the men."

Lewis took five men ashore with him to council with the now friendly chiefs, and after three hours Clark became concerned and sent a sergeant to check on Lewis. The sergeant returned with word that they were being treated well and had been invited to a dance in the evening. When Lewis finally returned, Clark went ashore and was presented with an "elegent" painted buffalo robe and was carried by six men to the council house on a white robe. He immediately told the chiefs that they would have to give up the Maha Indian slaves they had recently taken in a raid. The chiefs presented Clark with about 400 pounds of buffalo meat; one made an eloquent speech which Clark assumed agreed with his pleas for peace under the rule of the Great White Father. Then they passed the peace pipe around, and an Indian "took in one hand some of the most Delicate parts of the Dog which was prepared for the fiest and made a Sacrefise to the flag." They ate cooked dog meat, pemmican made of buffalo and fat, and ground potatoes.

After the meal, the dancing began with men singing and beating on tambourines and the women "highly Deckerated in their Way, with the Scalps and Tropies of War." He noted that women weren't much good at dancing, only jumping up and down, and that the five or six young men singing made up the words as they went (a far cry from Italian opera).

The following morning Clark wrote that he had had a bad night's sleep and woke to find the bank "as useal lined with Spectators." They handed out some more gifts, including blankets. Lewis again went ashore with a group of chiefs, while Clark stayed aboard the boats to write a letter to Old Dorian and to prepare some certificates and medals for the Tetons, and in midsentence he mentioned that when someone close died, "they run arrows through their flesh above and below their elbows as a testimony of their Grief."

Clark later went ashore and was treated to a repeat of the dance that still failed to impress him, in part because the poles they used in the dances were decorated with scalps.

When Lewis and Clark returned to the boats, a chief and his bodyguard accompanied them in a pirogue. The man steering was unaccustomed to the job and ran across the bow of the keelboat and snapped the anchor line, setting it adrift. Clark yelled at the men to man the oars, and the confusion frightened the Indians. The chief halloed to the rest of the tribe and the bank was again lined with unsmiling Indians.

After matters were again in hand and the Indians calm, the chief insisted that he and his bodyguard remain aboard that night as guests. The captains didn't say no, although they wanted to, nor was much sleep possible that night. To make matters worse, they could not find the anchor, so the keelboat was tied up close to shore, close enough for mischief should the Indians wish to try.

They continued the search for the anchor the next day but were unsuccessful, and "with great difficuelty" got the Indians off the boat and back to shore. When they tried to cast off and proceed on their journey, the Indian braves called "soldiers" grabbed the cable and would not let go. They demanded tobacco in return for letting them leave, and Lewis "would not agree to be forced into anything." Finally Clark threw some tobacco to them and pointed the port swivel cannon toward the shore as a means of reasoning with the chief. It worked. The chief gave the tobacco to his soldiers and "jurked the rope from them and handed it to the bowsman we then Set out under a Breeze from the S.E."

After they had gone upriver about two miles one of the chiefs, to whom Lewis and Clark had assigned numbers — in this case the third one — was seen on the shore beckoning to them. When they pulled over and took him aboard he explained that a "Double Spoken" chief had given the order to keep them from leaving. Soon they saw another Indian, the son of the chief who was aboard, so they took him on, too. They gave them a message for the rest of the Teton Sioux, that they should stay at home if they were in favor of peace and if they attacked the party, they were ready to defend themselves. They continued upriver for another hour-and-a-half, then pulled to shore to construct a new anchor of stones and to camp overnight because, as Clark wrote, "I am verry unwell for want of Sleep Deturmined to Sleep to night if possible, the Men Cooked & we rested well."

Their standoff with the Teton Sioux stood them in good stead as the journey progressed. Word of the adventure and of their coolness under pressure traveled ahead of them via the "moccasin telegraph" and when they arrived at the Arikara, or "Ree," Indian villages in northern South Dakota nearly two weeks later, they were given a royal welcome. Unlike the other Plains tribes they had encountered thus far, the Arikaras had an entirely different language, dwelled the year round in earthen lodges, and were primarily farmers rather than hunters and raiders.

Their lodges were built of a framework of large posts and cottonwood poles. Then a layer of willow branches was placed on the frame and covered with clay. The lodges were from thirty to forty feet in diameter and very cozy, no matter what the season. Each family's string of horses and dogs usually shared the lodges with them to avoid being stolen. Apparently the major danger in living that way was heavy rainfall, which could turn the lodges into wet poles with stacks of mud beneath them. Fortunately, the High Plains has a semiarid climate and only occasional repairs were due to this disadvantage.

The Arikaras were merchants, and other tribes would come hundreds of miles to trade for the crops of corn, beans, tobacco, squash, and melons the tribe grew.

The Arikaras were also the first tribe which the explorers met who had no desire for liquor. But this did not mean they possessed higher morals, by white man standards, than did the other tribes. They were sexually promiscuous and venereal discase was a major problem.

Mention of Clark's "servant," York, is seldom and brief in the journals, and one of the most revealing ones so far as Clark's attitude toward him is concerned was his October 10 comments about the Indians' reaction to York:

"Those Indians wer much astonished at my Servant, they never Saw a black man before, all flocked around him & examind him from top to toe, he Carried on the joke and made himself more turribal than we wished him to doe." In other words, one assumes, York was also having fun.

Three days later it was John Newman's turn to get in trouble. Most of the problems with the crew occurred early in the trip, during the settling-in period so to speak, and with the arrival of fall they were a relatively integrated and smoothly functioning crew. But Newman was confined for "mutinous expression." That night he was tried by court-martial for "having uttered repeated expressions of a highly criminal and mutinous nature, etc.," and he was sentenced to receive seventy-five lashes and to be disbanded from the party. The latter part of the punishment meant he would spend the winter with the party as would Reed, and both would return to St. Louis with the keelboat the following spring.

However, Newman's punishment was the last of its kind on the trip. The crew had settled down to work.

The Arikaras thought the lashing of Newman was barbaric. Early on the afternoon of Sunday, October 14, the party stopped at a sand bar in the river to administer the flogging, and the chief traveling with them into Mandan country "cried aloud (or effected to cry)" and told Clark after the punishment was explained that he "also thought examples were necessary, & he himself had made them by Death, his nation never whiped even their Children, from their burth."

From this point to the Mandan villages, the explorers almost daily had contact with Indians of various tribes, and the weather steadily degenerated from autumn to winter. They still "set out early" most mornings, but now they were finding ice on puddles of water and frost on the grass and their equipment, and rain often turned to sleet and hail. Clark was struck down by an attack of "Rhumetism in the neck which was So violent I could not move." Lewis applied a "hote stone wrapped in flanner" to give him some relief, but the next day he complained of frequent spasms of pain even while commenting on the surrounding country and the peculiar habits of Indians. Perhaps one should

Cannonball stones, North Dakota, for which Lewis and Clark named the river

say lack of habits in one case because they found some Indians who wore only a breechcloth in the freezing rain.

Their progress was frequently slowed by stops along the river to council or just chat with the Indians. Clark remarked that they went a whole day without seeing game along the river, a sure sign that the Indians were hunting nearby. They met the son of a chief who had recently died, and the son had chopped off two of his fingers, as was the tribal custom.

"The wind blew verry hard this evening from the S.W verry cold R. Fields with the Rhumatism in his neck, P. Crusat with the Same conplaint in his Legs — the party other wise is well, as to my self I feel but slight Simptoms of that disorder at this time." In other words, everything considered, Clark believed the trip was still going well.

Finally, on October 24, 1804, they arrived at the place they had chosen for winter quarters. By their reckoning they had traveled 1,600 miles since the previous May and they were at a site about sixty miles north of present-day Bismarck, North Dakota, among the Mandans at last. There were other Indians represented as well, mainly Minitaris and Amahamis, and they lived together for common protection from the Sioux. The explorers rated the population of the five villages at 4,400, the largest concentration of Indians on the Missouri River at that time. They were primarily farmers, and the Minitaris were the hunters of the group, often ranging far into present-day Montana for buffalo and other plains game.

After they had been among the tribes for a little more than a week, Lewis and Clark began seriously looking for a place for winter quarters. They wanted to stay some distance from the Indians, but not so far away that they would be unable to trade with them during the winter and gather whatever information they had about the rest of the journey. They finally selected a site seven or eight miles below the mouth of the Knife River on the east bank of the Missouri. The place Clark found was beneath tall bluffs in a wooded bottom with cottonwood, that indispensable tree of the expedition, which measured as much as eighteen inches in diameter. They immediately set to work building a fort, carpenter Gass being in charge. It was roughly triangular with two rows of huts joined at one point with a small tower for a sentry post. The front side was a palisade of tall posts with a low gate, facing the river.

The fort was completed on Christmas Day, but the men had occupied it back in mid-November as each hut was completed. Ice had started running in the river only a few days after their arrival, and snow was falling. They were settled in for the six-month-long winter at the edge of the unknown, their first winter on the trail but certainly not their last.

3

Winter Among the Mandans

"Some Snow to day, 8 men go to hunt the buffalow, killed a hare & wolf Several Indians visit us to day & a Gross Ventre came after his wife, who had been much abused, & came here for Protection."

An island with cottonwood *(Populus deltoides occidentalis)*

This entry by the observant but succinct Clark pretty well sums up the winter's activities at Fort Mandan. Food was a continuing problem because the roughly forty-five members of the Corps of Discovery could keep eight to ten hunters busy every day bringing in fresh game. They were camped far enough away from the Indians to keep them from getting underfoot constantly, but not so far away that they were immune to almost daily visitors. They had ample supplies of cottonwoood for the fires and enough left over to build some crude furniture.

The North Dakota winters were so severe, with wind and plunging temperatures, that in their journal entries the captains were soon commenting on warm mornings when it was only 28° above zero. Since it fell to 45° below zero on one occasion and stayed 20° below on several other days, 4° below freezing would seem balmy.

The captains kept busy with their journals, incorporating notes they had taken on the upriver trip; getting the specimens of plants and animals ready to send back to Washington with the keelboat the following spring; holding council with the Indians frequently, in part through courtesy and in part to learn as much about the rest of the Missouri River as possible; treating the sick and injured; and interviewing men to join them for the rest of the trip.

They made voluminous notes about the Indians' language, customs, and the land around them. They did considerable work on a vocabulary, but most of their work in linguistics was lost after the expedition ended.

One of the most important men at Mandan was John Shields, a talented blacksmith. The expedition already was low on trade goods, especially blue beads, and they wanted corn and other

Pocket gopher *(Thomomys talpoides rufescens)*

50

vegetables from the Indians. When the Indians discovered Shields' talents, they began showing up with a wide range of broken implements for him to repair. He did so in exchange for the needed food.

Then one of the warriors asked Shields to construct an iron battle-ax, which the journals call a spontoon, and Shields soon was in business fashioning a frightening array of weaponry for the Indians. When winter ended, the expedition had all the corn it wanted.

Undoubtedly the most valuable member of the expedition was the half-breed, Drouillard. Not only was he the most trustworthy, he was the best hunter, the best shot, and the coolest head under pressure. Whenever the leaders needed a man for a tough job, that of Drouillard (or Drewyer as they spelled his name) appeared in the journal entry for that day. During the Mandan winter, Drouillard was hardly ever around the fort during the day; he was always out in charge of a group of hunters, and the party never went hungry.

A battleax head of the kind Shields made during the Mandan winter

But providing food was a major undertaking, and students of the expedition have determined that it took the equivalent of a buffalo a day to keep the members of the group adequately fed. Since this requirement obviously could not be met every day, the difference had to be made up with the meat of deer, wolf, rabbit, elk, and whatever else they could glean from the rolling prairie around them.

Because the hunting around the Mandan villages was so intense and limited to a small area by the severe winter, the game natually thinned as winter progressed, and the hunters had to go farther afield, often staying out overnight. Sometimes they were out several days, in which case they often had to eat what they killed rather than bring it back. Clark wrote of returning with a party after walking thirty miles on ice and snow that was knee-deep, and of the men blistering and tearing their feet in thin moccasins as they walked over the knife-edged river ice.

As if this were not enough, there was always danger of running into hostile Sioux on the hunts, and Drouillard did just that earlier. The party of about 100 Sioux took their knives and horses but generously left the explorers' scalps intact.

Yet, there was enough to eat, thanks in part to Drouillard's skill and the trading that went on between the explorers and the Mandans, and the journals make no mention of grumbles among the meat eaters when they were forced to become — at least temporarily — vegetarians.

The captains had their share of illnesses to treat during the long winter, both among the party and among the nearby Indians. Several men fell ill and the standard procedure was, of course, to make a cut and let some of the "bad blood" flow out. All of the men survived this treatment, including Drouillard. Others suffered from frostbite, usually on the feet and hands.

The standard treatment for frostbite, which persisted until well into the middle of this century, was to submerge frostbitten parts in cold water and rub them with snow, which is just the reverse of the treatment given now, which is to immerse the frostbitten part in warm water to bring the temperature back to normal and to avoid rubbing it and causing severe injury to the skin and tissue.

One of the most difficult medical tasks Lewis had to undertake during the winter was the amputation of a young Indian's toes. He came to Fort Mandan after spending a night under a buffalo robe with both feet frozen. After a few days they found it necessary to take the toes off one foot. Of course no anesthesia was used because none was available and after the toes had been removed, the surfaces were then seared, or cauterized, with a hot iron.

Another peculiar chore for the medically trained Lewis was assisting in the birth of Sacajawea's son. The captain earlier had hired a French-Canadian trader named René Jusseaume and a former employee of the North-West Fur Company, Toussaint Charbonneau, as interpreters. The former had lived among the Knife River Indians several years and spoke several languages. Charbonneau also spoke the languages, and at that time had two Indian wifes, "two Squars of the Rock [Rocky] mountains, purchased from the Indians." Nothing further was said about the second wife, but one, a Shoshoni from the Bitterroot Valley of Montana who had been captured by the Hidatsas, was the famous Sacajawea.

At that time she was sixteen- or seventeen-years-old and in a state of advanced pregnancy. When she went into labor, Lewis described the event and the medicine used, making it clear that he did not actually deliver the baby as some writers since have insisted:

"about five Oclock this evening one of the wives of Charbono was delivered of a fine boy. it is worthy of remark that this was the first child which this woman had boarn, and as is common in such cases her labour was tedious and the pain violent; Mr. Jessome informed me that he had freequently administerd a small portion of the rattle of the rattle-snake, which he assured me had never failed to produce the desired effect, that of hastening the birth of the child; having the rattle of a snake by me I gave it to him and he administered two rings of it to the woman broken in small pieces with the fingers and added to a small quantity of water. Whether this medicine was truly the cause or not I shall not undertake to determine, but I was informed that she had not taken it more than ten minutes before she brought forth perhaps this remedy may be worthy of future experiments, but I must confess that I want faith as to its efficacy."

The matter of Sacajawea has long been a bone of contention among students of the expedition. Romanticists have tried to convert her into something of a Joan of Arc or the patron saint of the journey to the Pacific and back. The realists, working from the evidence at hand, have often found themselves accused of male chauvinism and other cardinal sins because they simply tried to place her in her proper context within the expedition.

There is no doubt that she was a pleasant traveling companion and useful many times. The men, particularly Clark, liked her very much, and her child, Baptiste — whom they nicknamed Little Pomp — was probably spoiled by the men. But Sacajawea was not a burden to the party and her knowledge of natural foods came in handy several times, as did her very presence; tribes met along the way instinctively knew the explorers' intentions were not warlike when they saw a woman with a baby accompanying them. And her contribution when they met the Shoshonis was incalculable.

Lewis expressed amazement at the treatment of horses by the Mandans, with whom they bartered for pack and saddle animals during the winter. When Drouillard returned from a trip on February 12, 1805, the day after Little Pomp was born, Lewis noted that the horses seemed "much fatieged" and ordered that they be fed some meal bran moistened with a little water, "but to my astonisment found that they would not eat it but prefered the bark of the cotton wood which forms the principall article of food usually given them by their Indian masters in the winter season; for this purpose they cause the tree to be felled by their women and the horses feed on the boughs and bark of their tender branches. the Indians in our neighbourhood are fre-

Interior of a Mandan lodge

quently pilfered of their horses by the Recares, Siouxs and Assinniboins and therefore make it an invariable rule to put their horses in their lodges at night. In this situation the only food of the horse consists of a few sticks of the cottonwood from the size of a man's finger to that of his arm.''

In addition to the business of simply staying alive and healthy during the long winter, the captains spent as much time as possible learning about the country ahead. Their best source was the group of Hidatsas encamped there because they ranged more widely than the other tribes, venturing far into the Rocky Mountains during the summers. They spent many hours in the lodges listening to descriptions of the upper Missouri and learning the streams that enter it along the way. They first heard of

Exterior of Mandan earthen huts

the grizzly bear from these Indians and from the information gleaned from several such conversations, Clark drew a map that is surprising in its accuracy. Some of the information was, of course, sketchy and much was lost in the process of interpretation. They were confused later at the mouth of the Marias, which the Indians called "the river that scolds all others," and they were in for a shock when they discovered that the portage around the Great Falls of the Missouri would become a major undertaking rather than a temporary inconvenience.

4

Fort Mandan to the Bitterroots

Toward the end of February, 1805 the men were engaged in cutting the pirogues and keelboat loose from the ice, which they

expected to begin moving by April. After two days' work, they
had the pirogues loose but the keelboat was a more difficult
task. By March 2, the ice was breaking up in earnest and on
March 5 the temperature was up to 40° and the Indians were out
burning the plains to induce an early crop of grass for the buffalo
and their horses.

Black-billed mag-pie *(Pica pica hud-sonia)*

The month of March was devoted to final preparations for the
resumption of the journey and to loading the keelboat for the
return trip to St. Louis. They were already having some
problems with Charbonneau, whose presence was never as
pleasant or useful as that of his teenage wife. Clark wrote that he
had been "corrupted" by a fur company (he declined to name it
in the journals) and was uncertain if the interpreter would accompany them. Charbonneau refused to work or stand guard
and "if miffed with any man he wishes to return when he
pleases, also have the disposal of as much provisions as he
Chuses to Carry."

Clark itemized the "Sundrey articles" to be sent to the President of the United States aboard the keelboat:

Male and female antelope skeletons and skins, horns of two
mule — or black-tailed — deer, Mandan bow and quiver of
arrows, tobacco seed, marten skin, mule deer tail, a weasel,
three squirrels, bones and skeleton of a coyote, a white and gray
hare skeleton, 4 buffalo robes, an ear of corn, male and female
prairie dog, tobacco, red fox skin, a magpie, some articles of
Indian dress, 13 red fox skins, mountain ram horns, a robe with
pictures representing a battle between the Sioux and Arikaras
against the Mandans and Minitaris.

A Mandan chief

Also, the skins and skeletons of female and male antelopes, a
bear skin (called a Yellow bear in the inventory, thus apparently
the cinnamon-colored grizzly which became a recognized sub-
species), numerous specimens of plants ranging from seed to
pressed and dried leaves to the whole plant, Mandan pottery,
and mice and insects.

Included in the shipment were three cages containing a prairie
dog, four magpies, and a prairie sharp-tailed grouse, all being
shipped out live.

By April 5 they had the two pirogues and six canoes loaded
and ready, the latter new to the Corps of Discovery's complement. With departure imminent, the Indians became friendlier
and the bartering more intense. The women were even more
available than before, and York remained popular among the

A Mandan trophy

Bearberry *(Arctostapnylos uva-ursi),* pressed by Lewis at Fort Mandan

women. His black skin had been a curiosity all along the river, as it would continue to be throughout the voyage, and obtaining female companionship was never a problem for the slave. Nothing was said in the journals about his relationship with the rest of the crew, but since he was a slave, we must assume he was treated as such. Most of Clark's comments about him reveal the patronizing attitude common between master and slave, and it is interesting — and ironic on Clark's part — to note that the captains negotiated with the Indians, trying to make them relinquish their slaves. Perhaps Clark didn't really consider York to be a slave, since he referred to him as a servant and permitted him to have a personality of sorts in the journals. But York was not a free man, and he was very low in the expedition's pecking order.

On April 7, 1805, the keelboat, or barge as Lewis called it, was sent back to St. Louis with a crew of six soldiers, two French traders, and an Indian going downriver to the next encampment. Corporal Richard Warfington was in charge of the keelboat, and one of the Frenchmen, Joseph Gravelines, was hired as the pilot.

"Our vessels consisted of six small canoes, and two large perogues," Lewis wrote. "This little fleet altho' not quite so rispectable as those of Columbus or Capt. Cook, were still viewed by us with much pleasure as those deservedly famed adventurers ever beheld theirs; and I dare say with quite as much anxiety for their safety and preservation.

"we were now about to penetrate a country at least two thousand miles in width, on which the foot of civilized man had never trodden; the good or evil it had in store for us was for experiment yet to determine, and these little vessells contained every article by which we were to expect to subsist or defend ourselves. however, as the state of mind in which we are, generally gives the colouring to the events, when the immagination is suffered to wander into futurity, the picture which now presented itself to me was a most pleasing one. entertaining as I do, the most confident hope of succeeding in a voyage which had formed a darling project of mine for the last ten years, I could but esteem this moment of my departure as among the most happy in my life. The party are in excellent health and sperits, zealously attached to the enterprise, and anxious to proceed; not a whisper of murmur or discontent to be heard among them, but all act in unison, and with the most perfect harmony."

Most of the journal entries from St. Louis to Fort Mandan had been made by Clark and it is uncertain if they combined their writings into one account, if Lewis' notes were lost, or if Lewis simply did not do any writing on the way upriver. But from Fort Mandan west Lewis did much of the writing, with occasional unexplained lapses, and there are frequent examples of his poetic turn of mind such as the one just quoted. Whereas Clark was the more straightforward writer, with frequent dashes of wit and good cheer, Lewis tended toward the more florid and emotional, even though his spelling and punctuation were not nearly so adventurous and full of surprises as Clark's.

On their very first day under way again (April 8), they had problems with the canoes. They faced a strong headwind out of the northwest and one of the canoes was soon half-filled with water. They lost half a bag of "bisquites" and about thirty pounds of powder. They pitched camp at the site of the accident, near present-day Hancock, North Dakota, and refused the affections of a Mandan woman whose husband brought her to camp for that purpose.

The next day the Indian who had signed on to accompany them to the Snake River decided he didn't want to go west after all and headed back downriver toward home. Lewis began writing longer and more detailed entries about the natural history of the plains, and his keen powers of observation and talent of selecting the most pertinent details to record have been the marvel of scientists and others. He would describe a species of animal, bird, or fish; write what he had heard about them from Indians and others; and then include his own observations about their habits and relevance to the whole ecosystem of the route. Later naturalists who have devoted almost their entire careers to studying the journals are virtually unanimous in their praise for both captains' scientific notes, particularly those of Lewis.

From the time the Indian left them just after setting off from Fort Mandan, they would be out of sight of Indians until they reached the headwaters of the Missouri in August, four months later. They traversed the entire state of Montana and part of North Dakota, some of the richest game areas in the West and entered what amounted to the "Freeway of the West," yet strangely, they saw no Indians. It has to be one of the most remarkable noncoincidences in Western history.

So they were under way again, healthy except for venereal outbreak among some of the men that Lewis and Clark mention almost casually in the journals when they gave treatments with mercury ointment. Dr. Drake W. Will, a physician writing about the expedition, suspected that Lewis administered a dose of calomel and jalap "to clear the bowels" ahead of the next medicine, calomel alone in pill form. This was given, he thought, until sore gums appeared and was then discontinued. After the gums healed, calomel was continued until the venereal sores disappeared.

This brings up another matter of debate among students of the expedition: were both Lewis and Clark celibate during the entire trip? We have no way of knowing because no evidence of amorous escapades by either leader is mentioned in the journals, neither those kept by the leaders nor those kept by the six enlisted men that have survived. There are liberal mentions of the other men succumbing to the charms of Indian women along the route, but nothing about Lewis or Clark. One wonders. . . .

During the first few days out they were faced with a potential shortage of game because the area had been so heavily hunted by the Indians. Lewis commented on that scourge of the Western states that continues to be a problem to travelers, namely, alkali, or more specifically, carbonate of soda. As Lewis wrote on April 11, "on the sides of the hills and even the banks of the rivers and sandbars, there is a white substance that appears in considerable quantities on the surface of the earth, which tastes like a mixture of common salt and glauber salts (named for a German chemist in the seventeenth century). many of the springs which flow from the base of the river hills are so strongly impregnated with this substance that the water is extreemly unpleasant to the taste and has a purgative effect.''

Parenthetically, when the author and his family traveled along the trail, they noticed the alkaline taste in the water of eastern Montana and the Dakotas, although they were not subjected to the purgative effect.

And on the same day Lewis commented on the water, Clark wrote that they found "Several Stratums of bituminious substance which resembles *coal*; though Some of the pieces appear to be excellent coal, it resists the fire for some time and consumes without emiting much flaim." At this writing, the vast coalfields just beneath the surface in eastern Montana are a source of major conflict among coal companies, ranchers, and the environmental protection organizations.

By this time the leaders had hit their stride as journalists and their entries are marvelously detailed and written with a deep appreciation for the countryside and their fellowship within the party, which by now was a smoothly functioning unit. Disciplinary problems were gone and the remainder of the trip was made with no serious personnel problems. They also knew they were entering a part of the continent white men had penetrated but rarely.

Although the weather was still brisk at times, with snow flurries and frosty mornings, and the strong and steady wind that has always swept the plains and thrown dirt in eyes, still this section of the trip — from Mandan to the Great Falls — was one of the most pleasant of the expedition. Once they left the Mandan area behind and food became plentiful again, the members of the expedition were practically on a spring outing across the plains with all the prairie colors out and the blue Rocky Mountains far ahead.

On April 14 they were near a creek which they named for Charbonneau, which was later renamed Indian Creek, when Lewis went out to shoot an elk. He saw the first grizzlies of the trip, a pair that, frightened by the shot, ran away. "Those animals assended those Steep hills with supprising ease & verlocity, they were too far to discover their prosise colour &

Audubon's
mountain sheep
(*Ovis canadensis
auduboni*)

size,'' Clark wrote. But they were to discover more than they had really cared to learn about the ''white bears'' before many days passed.

On the same day, Lewis commented on a large ''hooting owl'' one of the party members had killed. He saw little difference between it and the other hoot owls seen in the United States, ''except that this appeared to be more booted and more thickly clad with feathers.'' The bird later was identified as a sub-species called the Montana Horned Owl (*Bubo virginianus occidentalis*), and the site of its discovery (or death, whichever you prefer) was somewhere in Mountrail County, North Dakota.

Another species discovered was the Audubon Mountain Sheep (*Ovis Canadensis auduboni*) first spotted by Joseph Field on April 26 at the mouth of the Yellowstone. The discovery, and subsequent frequent sightings along the river all the way to the mountains, showed that it had a surprisingly wide range.

They continued to see signs of the grizzly, and on April 17 Lewis wrote his attitude toward the Mandans and the feared bear: ''tho' we continue to see many tracks of the bear we have seen but very few of them, and those are at a great distance generally runing away from us; I therefore presume that they are extreemly wary and shy; the Indian account of them dose not corrispond with our experience so far.''

On April 29 Lewis began his education on them:

''Set out this morning at the usual hour; the wind was moderate; I walked on shore with one man. about 8 A.M. we fell in with two brown or yellow (*white*) bear; both of which we wounded; one of them made his escape, the other after my firing on him pursued me seventy or eighty yards, but fortunately had been so badly wounded that he was unable to pursue so closely as to prevent my charging my gun; we again repeated our fire and killed him . . . these are all the particulars in which this anamal appeared to me to differ from the black bear; it is a much more furious and formidable anamal, and will frequently pursue the hunter when wounded. it is asstonishing to see the wounds they will bear before they can be put to death. the Indians may well fear this anamal equiped as they generally are with their bows and arrows of indifferent sizees, but in the hands of skillfull riflemen they are by no means as formidable or dangerous as they have been represented.''

Black bear *(Ursus americanus)*

Obviously, he had learned a little about the grizzlies, but not enough.

On May 5 they killed another bear:

"Capt. Clark and Drewyer [Drouillard] killed the largest brown bear this evening which we have ever seen. it is a most tremendious looking anamal, and extreemly hard to kill notwithstanding he had five balls through his lungs and five others in various parts he swam more than half the distance across the river to a sandbar, & it was at least twenty minutes before he died; he did not attempt to attack, but fled and made the most tremendous roaring from the moment he was shot."

But Tuesday, May 14, 1805, was a bad day. A very bad day. First, they tangled with another grizzly; Lewis described the action:

"In the evening the men in two of the rear canoes discovered a large brown bear lying in the open grounds about 300 paces from the river, and six of them went out to attack him, all good hunters; they took the advantage of a small eminence which concealed them and got within 40 paces of him unperceived, two of them reserved their fires as had been previously conscerted, the four others fired nearly at the same time and put each his bullet through him, two of the balls passed through the bulk of both lobes of his lungs, in an instant this monster ran at them with open mouth, the two who had reserved their fires discharged their pieces at him as he came towards them, boath of them struck him, one only slightly and the other fortunately broke his shoulder, this however only retarded his motion for a moment only, the men unable to reload their guns took flight, the bear pursued and had very nearly overtaken them before they reached the river; two of the party betook themselves to a canoe and the others separated and concealed themselves among the willows, reloaded their pieces, each discharged his

Grizzly bear *(Ursus horribilis)*

piece at him as they had an opportunity   they struck him several times again but the guns served only to direct the bear to them, in this manner he pursued two of them seperately so close that they were obliged to throw aside their guns and pouches and throw themselves in the river altho' the bank was nearly twenty feet perpendicular; so enraged was this anamal that he plunged into the river only a few feet behind the second man he compelled to take refuge in the water, when one of thse still remained on shore shot him through the head and finally killed him; they then took him on shore and butchered him when they found eight balls had passed through him in different directions."

After this episode — and there were other encounters with grizzlies — the explorers no longer doubted the Indians' warnings about the ferocity of the big creatures.

The day wasn't over yet. About the same time as the battle with the grizzly, another drama was being enacted in the boats. Both Lewis and Clark were on shore witnessing the near sinking of a pirogue with Charbonneau at the helm instead of Drouillard, who usually commanded it. Since they trusted Drouillard more than any of the other enlisted men, they had their papers, instruments, books, medicine, and a large load of trade goods in it.

When the pirogue was abreast of Lewis and Clark, with Charbonneau, Sacajawea, Little Pomp, and Cruzatte all aboard with the precious cargo, a sudden squall hit the river and Charbonneau, a nonswimmer, panicked. "The steersman allarmed," Lewis wrote, "instead of puting her before the wind, lufted her up into it, the wind was so violent that it drew the brace of the squarsail out of the hand of the man who was attending it, and instantly upset the perogue and would have turned her completely topsaturva, had it not have been from the resistance made by the oarning [awning] against the water."

The leaders stood helplessly on the bank, trying to shout instructions to the people in the boat who could not hear, and when they fired shots to attract their attention, apparently no one even heard that. To Lewis' and Clark's surprise the pirogue righted itself, even though it had gone all the way over on its side, but it came upright with the precious cargo immersed in half a boatload of water.

Charbonneau disgusted everyone by becoming helpless, and instead of trying to help bring the boat under control, Lewis wrote, "Charbono still crying to his god for mercy, had not yet recollected the rudder, nor could the repeated orders of the Bowsman, Cruzat, bring him to his recollection untill he threatened to shoot him instantly if he did not take hold of the rudder and do his duty."

Cruzatte saved the boat, and Sacajawea, who kept her wits about her, caught nearly all of the papers and other cargo that floated free when the pirogue took on water and with Cruzatte shouting dire threats, they were able to paddle to shore with the boat barely above the choppy water.

Lewis was so frightened at the prospect of losing the precious material that he once started to jump in and swim out to the pirogue but wisely changed his mind because he knew he could not swim 300 yards.

The next day Lewis wrote that the loss from the accident was relatively small, especially in light of what could have been lost. Several medical stores were completely destroyed as well as some garden seeds they had collected, and some gunpowder fell overboard and sank. Had they lost the entire cargo, the trip might have ended right then.

Almost as an afterthought, Lewis wrote that "a white bear toar Labuiche's coat which he had left in the plains."

By mid-May they were entering the rough, broken land of Montana that separates the Great Plains from the Rockies, and on May 21 they entered what is now called the Missouri Breaks, a dramatic area of towering sandstone and clay banks carved by wind and rain into fantastic formations. The river was swifter and shallower through that stretch as they passed more feeder streams, and the men were wearing out moccasins and leggings faster than before as they spent more time on shore pulling the boats upstream with towropes made from animal skins.

To increase their discomfort, the wind blew almost constantly, sometimes hard enough to delay them for several hours, and it was always strong enough to throw grit in their eyes. Game was still plentiful, but Lewis commented that they had caught very few fish since leaving Fort Mandan, and those few were white catfish weighing two to five pounds. The temperature was still low at night, sometimes low enough to freeze the edge of the river. They often sent men out away from the river to investigate the surrounding country, who invariably returned reporting only more of the same: broken land with many gullies, scrub pine, spruce, and some cedar on the hills. They saw many

The Missouri Breaks

thousands of buffaloes, and the bighorn sheep were almost as common as antelopes. Lewis made a detailed examination of sheep carcasses brought in, and as he did throughout the trip added the information he had acquired from Indians or the few white traders and trappers and then gave his own opinion of that information.

On May 26, Clark climbed out of the river crevice to the top of a knoll for his first look at the Rocky Mountains. "whilst I viewed those mountains I felt a secret pleasure in finding myself so near the head of the heretofore conceived boundless Missouri; but when I reflected on the difficulties which this snowey barrier would most probably throw in my way to the Pacific Ocean, and the sufferings and hardships of my self and the party

67

Channel catfish *(Ic-talurus punctatus)*

in them, it in some measure counterballanced the joy I had felt in the first moments in which I gazed on them; but as I have always held it little Short of criminality to anticipate evils I will allow it to be a good comfortable road untill I am compelled to believe otherwise.''

Here, perhaps more than in any other journal entry, we learn what kind of realistic optimist Clark really was.

Three days later the group was camped near a small creek that gave them good reason for naming it Bull Creek. A bull buffalo swam the Missouri that night and emerged from the river by climbing over one of the pirogues. As Lewis described it, ''he then allarmed ran up the bank in full speed directly towards the fires, and was within 18 inches of the heads of some of the men who lay sleeping before the centinel could allarm him or make him change his course, still more alarmed, he now took his direction immediately towards our lodge, passing between 4 fires and within a few inches of the heads of one range of the men as they lay sleeping, when he came near the tent, my dog saved us by causing him to change his course a second time, which he did by turning a little to the right, and was quickly out of sight.'' Lewis added that the scene he left behind was almost comical, with all the men being up and armed and asking each other what happened and where the beast went.

The next morning they found that the buffalo had stepped on a rifle belonging to ''Capt. Clark's black man who had negligently left her in the perogue, the rifle was much bent, he had also broken the spindle; pivit, and shattered the stock of one of the blunderbushes on board.''

That same day they passed the river that Lewis named the Bighorn, but which Clark later renamed the Judith, his nickname for Julia Hancock, a 13-year-old girl from Fincastle, Virginia, who later became his wife. Later in the day they towed the boats past a cliff over which Indians had driven buffalo to their death; it was one of the many famous buffalo jumps found throughout the northern plains. Lewis wrote at length about the buffalo jump, explaining that a young man fast on his feet was chosen to disguise himself as a buffalo by wearing a buffalo robe and head and to place himself near the edge of the cliff. The other Indians then rounded up the herd and drove it toward the disguised Indian, who started to run toward the cliff, the herd following. ''The part of the decoy I am informed is extreamly dangerous, if they are not very fleet runers the buffaloe tread

Buffalo jump in eastern Montana

them under foot and crush them to death, and sometimes drive them over the precipice also, where they perish in common with the buffaloe.''

They also saw many wolves feeding on the rotten carcasses and Clark was able to walk up to one and kill it with his ''espontoon,'' a lance-like weapon that could double as a walking staff. Small wonder that they named the nearby stream Slaughter River, which name has since been changed to Arrow Creek.

The Missouri River here is one of the stretches with no dams obstructing the flow of the river. And it is here that Lewis wrote one of his most beautifully descriptive passages in the journals. It is doubtful that anyone since has been as successful as he at describing the breaks in a way that is both technically accurate and emotionally responsive.

''The hills and river Clifts which we passed today exhibit a most romantic appearance. The bluffs of the river rise to the hight of from 2 to 300 feet and in most places nearly perpendicular; they are formed of remarkable white sandstone which is sufficiently soft to give way readily to the impression of water; two or three thin horizontal stratas of white freestone, on which the rains or water make no impression, lie imbeded in these clifts of soft stone near the upper part of them; the earth on the top of these Clifts is a dark rich loam, which forming a gradutly ascending plain extends back from ½ a mile to a mile where the hills commence and rise abruptly to a hight of about 300 feet or

Plains gray wolf *(Canis lupus nubilis)*

Detail of sandstone formation in Missouri Breaks

more. The water in the course of time in decending from those hills and plains on either side of the river has trickled down the soft sand clifts and woarn it into a thousand grotesque figures, which with the help of a little immagination and an oblique view, at a distance are made to represent eligant ranges of freestone buildings, having their parapets well stocked with statuary; Collumns of various sculpture both grooved and plain, are also seen supporting long galleries in front of those buildings; in other places on a much nearer approach and with the help of less imagination we see the remains or ruins of eligant buildings; some collumns standing and almost entire with their pedestals and capitals; others retaining their pedestals but deprived by time or accident of their capitals, some lying prostrate an broken others in the form of vast pyramids of conic structure bearing a serees of other pyramids on their tops becoming less as they ascend and finally terminating in a sharp point. nitches and alcoves of various forms and sizes are seen at different hights as we pass. a number of small martin which build their nests with clay in a globular form attached to the wall within those nitches, and which were seen hovering about the tops of the collumns did not the less remind us of some of those large stone buildings in the U. States. the thin stratas of hard freestone intermixed with the soft sandstone seems to have aided the water in forming this curious scenery. As we pass on it seemed as if those seens of visionary inchantment would never have and [an] end; for here it is too that nature presents to the view of the traveler vast ranges of walls of tolerable workmanship, so perfect indeed are those walls that I should have thought that nature had attempted here to rival the human art of masonry had I not recollected that she had first began her work . . ."

It was in these fantastic cliffs that Lewis also saw what he considered to be one of the most beautiful animals of the trip, a fox that he thought was orange-yellow with black and white markings. It apparently was a variety of the common red fox so prized by trappers, a cross-fox with markings on the back similar to a cross.

As they progressed upriver through the Breaks, they saw less timber and more signs of Indians, especially abandoned lodge poles. They also saw and commented both on the plant life that was emerging at the end of May and (occasionally) on the outcroppings of coal along the river.

There was little, if any, paddling upriver now. The river was so shallow and swift that they had to pull the crafts up with towropes made of elk and buffalo hide, and the frequent rains kept the river bank so slippery and sticky that men were constantly plagued by lost moccasins.

Cliff swallows (*Petrochelidon pyrrhonota*)

On June 3, 1805, they reached the junction of two large rivers and a dilemma: Which river was the true Missouri?

It was a question that took them nine days to settle. Lewis was well aware of the time element the day they arrived at what is now the Marias River, and he fretted over the possibility of either taking the wrong fork and having to retrace the route and being caught by winter in the mountains, or just wasting the precious summer trying to establish the proper route.

The captains sent out parties both by canoe and on foot to follow both streams in order to prove which branch was the true Missouri. Each group was instructed to make day trips only, while other members of the party dressed skins for clothing. Many of the men's feet were mangled by the stones over which they had walked, barefoot in some cases.

But the problem of the streams vexed the party more than did physical discomforts. Lewis made a careful study of both streams and wrote that the north river, the Marias, ran in a similar fashion to the Missouri below the confluence — the same "boiling and roling manner" — and its color was the same "whitish brown . . . very thick and terbid . . . in short the air & character of this river is so precisely that of the missouri below that the party with very few exceptions have already pronounced the N. fork to be the Missouri; myself and Capt. C. not quite so percipitate have not yet decided but if we were to give our opinions I believe we should be in the minority."

Yet they stayed in the camp at the confluence and continued to send out scouting parties for definite proof of which fork to take. The rain fell almost daily, keeping the river bank a quagmire and making walks along the bluffs dangerous. On June 7, Lewis and a private, Windsor, had a narrow escape while on an outing. Traversing a narrow ledge about thirty feet long that dropped off ninety feet to rocks below, Lewis almost fell but was able to catch himself by using his spontoon; however, he had no sooner crossed the ledge to safety than he heard Windsor shouting for help behind him.

Windsor had slipped, also, and was about halfway across the ledge lying flat on his belly with his right hand and leg over the side while holding on with his left arm and leg. Lewis said he expected to see him slip over the edge at any moment, but he spoke to him calmly and told him to take his knife out of his belt and use it to dig a hole in the bank for his right foot. Windsor did as he was told and crawled across the rest of the bank on his hands and knees.

On June 8, in spite of the frustration the river caused them, Lewis gave it the name of Maria's River, in honor of Maria Wood, his cousin. By doing so, he tacitly announced to the rest of the party that it was not the true Missouri. He wrote that the rest of the party was still of the definite opinion that they should follow it even though it swung farther north than the Indians at Mandan had told them. But Lewis and Clark stuck to their plan, or perhaps it was a hunch, while praising the Marias as being the possible entrance into the fur region then controlled by the British in Canada. They were so certain the Marias offered an easy gateway into the north country that they planned then to explore it more thoroughly on the return journey.

The decision being made to follow the left-hand river, the party was put to work caching some of the boats and cargo for the return trip the following year. They hid one of the pirogues, the large red one, "and all the heavy baggage which we could possibly do without and some provisions, salt, tools powder and Lead &c with a view to lighten our vessels,'' Lewis wrote. ''On enquiry I found that Cruzatte was well acquainted (with) this business (of digging caches) and therefore left the management of it entirely to him.''

The caches dug by Cruzatte and his crew resembled the old-fashioned cisterns used until recently by many farmers and ranchers. The opening was relatively narrow, and a few feet down the walls were dug outward so that the hole resembled a squat-shaped bottle. After the cache was put in and wrapped in buffalo and deer hides and mounted on sticks for drainage, it was covered and the sod replaced on top. That evening they capped off their days of frustration on the Marias by having Cruzatte play some music on his violin ''and the men passed the evening in dancing singing &c and were extreemly cheerfull.''

They stayed at the camp three more days, working on the caches and recovering from a variety of illnesses that afflicted Lewis and Sacajawea. On June 11, feeling much better, Lewis left overland with a small party composed of Drouillard, Joseph Field, Gibson, and Goodrich, in search of the Great Falls. Clark and the rest stayed in camp another day, in part because Sacajawea was too ill to travel and Clark had to administer that frontier cure-all known as bleeding.

Before noon of the second day out, Lewis' party heard the great roaring of the falls. They walked a little farther and saw spray rising from them like ''a collumn of smoke.'' When they

The Great Falls of the Missouri

Cutthroat trout
(Salmo Clarkii)

arrived at the falls, Lewis hurried down a hill to a rock "to gaze on this sublimely grand specticle."

He wrote about 500 words describing the falls, then had second thoughts: "after wrighting this imperfect discription I again viewed the falls and was so much disgusted with the imperfect idea which it conveyed of the scene that I determined to draw my pen across it and begin agin, but then reflected that I could not perhaps succeed better than pening the first impressions of the mind." Later writers following in his footsteps along the route can appreciate his feeling of inadequacy.

That evening Lewis dined on "buffaloe's humps, tongues and marrow-bones, fine trout parched meal pepper and salt, and a good appetite; the last is not considered the least of the luxuries," he wrote in reference to his recent illness with an upset stomach.

Meanwhile, back at the Clark camp, life was far from boring. Sacajawea was extremely ill and Clark, who became so attached to her that some romanticists have tried to prove they had a love affair, said "her case is somewhat dangerous." He also had two men with toothaches, two with tumors, and one with both a tumor and a slight fever. He gave Sacajawea a potion of boiled bark and applied a poultice to her midriff. Her husband, the virtually worthless Charbonneau, added to the general irritation by wanting the party to turn back and head downriver.

Lewis was simultaneously involved in another adventure with a grizzly. All men on a two-year adventure leave their guard down on occasion, but Lewis appears to have had a knack of leaving his down at the worst possible time. One such incident occurred on June 14, while he and his small crew were scouting a portage route around the series of falls that constitute the Great Falls.

He had just shot a fat buffalo through the lungs and "while I was gazeing attentively on the poor anamal discharging blood in streams from his mouth and nostrils, expecting him to fall every instant, and having entirely forgotten to reload my rifle, a large white, or reather brown bear, had perceived and crept up on me within 20 steps before I discovered him; in the first moment I drew up my gun to shoot, but at the same instant recolected that she was not loaded and that he was too near for me to hope to perform this operation before he reached me, as he was then briskly advancing on me; it was an open level plain, not a bush within miles nor a tree within less than three hundred yards of me; the river bank was sloping and not more than three feet above the level of the water; in short there was no place by means of which I could conceal myself from this monster untill I could charge my rifle; in this situation I thought of retreating in a brisk walk as fast as he was advancing until I could reach a tree about 300 yards below me, but I had no sooner terned myself about but he pitched at me, open mouthed and full speed, I ran about 80 yards and found he gained on me fast, I then run into the water . . . the idea struck me to get into the water to such depth that I could stand and he would be obliged to swim, and that I could in that situation defend myself with my espontoon; accordingly I ran haistily into the water about waist deep. and faced about and presented the point of my espontoon, at this instant he arrived at the edge of the water within about 20 feet of me; the moment I put myself in this attitude of defence he sudonly wheeled about as if frightened, declined the combat on such unequal grounds, and retreated with quite as great precipitation as he had just before pursued me.''

Lewis returned to shore and reloaded his gun and watched the grizzly, still running full bore, as he disappeared over a hill some three miles away, occasionally looking back over his shoulder to see if Lewis were after him.

His spirits reviving after the bear charged off into the wilderness, Lewis later in the day took a shot at a feline that was either a cougar or a wolverine and missed and then faced down three bull buffalo that charged him from half a mile away. ''I thought at least to give them some amusement and altered my direction to meet them,'' he wrote. They halted about a hundred yards from him, looked him over, and then turned and ran again in the direction from which they came. Lewis was feeling pretty good about the day, all things considered, since he had frightened a grizzly, possibly a cougar, and three buffalo. But he didn't care to push his luck much further.

''I then continued my rout homewards passed the buffaloe which I had killed, but did not think it prudent to remain all night at this place which really from the succession of curious adventures wore the impression on my mind of inchantment; at sometimes for a moment I thought it might be a dream, but the prickley pears which pierced my feet very severely once in a while, particularly after it grew dark, convinced me that I was really awake.''

He arrived back at camp long after dark to find the men very worried about him; some of them were convinced he had been killed.

After the long delay at the Marias River, they were faced with another almost as long at the Great Falls. Clark had some experience in surveying and mapmaking, so he set out to mark a trail around the series of falls. The route was roughly eighteen miles across the barren flats covered with sharp rocks and low-growing cactus, and it went through what is now Malmstrom Air Force Base and the southern part of the city of Great Falls.

Since it was impractical, if not impossible, to haul the baggage and canoes over the route on their backs, and since they had not encountered any Indians from whom to buy packhorses, the only alternative was to build some extremely crude wagons, hitch the men to them, and pull them across the rough, broken ground. Lewis supervised the construction of the two wagons with wheels made from a cottonwood tree they felled that was about twenty-two inches in diameter. Parts of the tree were used for tongues, couplings, frames, and braces, and the mast from the remaining pirogue was used for axles.

In the meantime, Sacajawea slowly improved and the explorers declared the cure was water brought to her from a sulfur spring a short distance upriver from the lower portage camp they had established. But in their journals both expedition leaders continually harangued her husband about how he did not take proper care of her. When she was finally able to walk again, she "walked out and gathered a considerable quantity of the white apples of which she ate so heartily in their raw state, together with a considerable quantity of dried fish without my knowledge that she complained very much and her fever again returned. I rebuked Sharbono severely for suffering her to indulge herself with such food he being privy to it and having been previously told what she must only eat," Lewis complained. In other journal entries Lewis seemed of divided concerns about Sacajawea; he didn't want her to be ill, of course, but one of the main reasons was her usefulness when they reached the Bitterroots and her own people. Clark was much more open with his concern: he pitied her for her suffering and was worried about Little Pomp.

Clark finished surveying a route for the portage and had the men drive stakes in the ground to mark the trail. On Saturday, June 22, 1805, they struck out with the first load over the trail, leaving behind Ordway, Charbonneau (who refused to work), Goodrich, York, and Sacajawea. They covered about eight miles before stopping to have lunch and to replace both axle trees, the tongues, and the hubs of a set of wheels. They replaced them with willow, which was no better than cottonwood had been and when night fell, they were still short of their goal, and the wagon had broken down again. Lewis wrote that each man took as much baggage as he could carry and "proceeded to the river where we formed our encampment much fortiegued. the prickly pears were extreemly troublesome to us sticking out feet through our mockersons."

The next day Lewis decided to put his pet project to the test. He had been carrying in the baggage the metal pieces of a knockdown canoe he called "The Experiment." He had had it constructed to his specifications at Harpers Ferry, Virginia and brought it down the Ohio River with him, all the way to Great Falls. While the party was working terribly hard on the portage, and men were often falling in their tracks from utter exhaustion, Lewis was spending part of his time and energy on an idea the time for which had not yet come.

The iron frame was thirty-six feet long, had both iron and wood struts and was covered with a variety of elk and buffalo skins sewn together, The basic problem was that there was no sealant for the seams; however, Lewis concocted a mixture of crushed charcoal, buffalo tallow and beeswax. After the portaging was over, Lewis launched the canoe and it floated like a cork. The next morning unfortunately, it was floating like an anchor because the seams had parted and it sat on the bottom of the river. Thoroughly "mortifyed," Lewis abandoned the idea and the expedition was held up another five days in constructing two dugouts of cottonwood in place of the Experiment.

The Great Falls portage was without doubt the most uncomfortable stretch of trail they had to traverse. The Bitterroots was rough, no doubt, and they had to go without food for much of that journey. But for sheer discomfort — and unrelenting pain — the portage was a section of trail the men did not care to repeat. No mutterings of mutiny were recorded in the journals, but they must surely have been thought.

In the midst of the portaging, Clark had a very close call with

Mother Nature. With York, Charbonneau, Sacajawea, and Little Pomp he went that fine Saturday, June 29, to retrieve a load of baggage.

"soon after I arrived at the falls, I perceived a cloud which appeared black and threaten imediate rain, I looked out for a shelter but could see no place without being in great danger of being blown into the river if the wind should prove as turbelant as it is at some times   about ¼ of a mile above the falls I obsd. a Deep riveen in which there was shelveing rocks under which we took shelter near the river and placed our guns the compass &c.&c. under a shelving rock on the upper side of the creek, in a place which was verry secure from rain, the first shower was moderate accompanied with a violent wind, the effects of which we did not feel   soon after a torrent of rain and hail fell more violent than ever I saw before, the rain fell like one voley of water falling from the heavens and gave us time to get out of the way of a torrent of water which was Poreing down the hill into the River with emence force tareing everything before it takeing with it large rocks & mud, I took my gun & shot pouch in my left hand, and with the right scrambled up the hill pushing the Interpreters wife (who had her child in her arms) before me, the Interpreter himself makeing attempts to pull up his wife by the hand much scared and nearly without motion, we at length reached the top of the hill safe where I found my servent in serch of us greatly agitated, for our wellfar. before I got out of the bottom of the reveen which was a flat dry rock when I entered it, the water was up to my waste & wet my watch, I scercely got out before it raised 10 feet deep with a torrent which was turrouble to behold, and by the time I reached the top of the hill, at least 15 feet water, I derected the party to return to the camp at the run as fast as possible to get out Lode where Clothes could be got to cover the child whose clothes were all lost, and the woman who was but just recovering from a severe indisposition, and was wet and cold, I was fearfull of a relaps   I caused her as also the other of the party to take a little spirits, which my servent had in a canteen, which revived (them) verry much."

Evidently the party was not prudish about nudity because when Clark's group returned to camp, the others "had returned in great confusion to the run leaveing their loads in the Plain, the hail & wind being so large and violent in the plains, and them naked, they were much brused, and some nearly killed one knocked down three times, and others without hats or anything

Bald eagle *(Haliaeetus leucocephalus)*

on their heads bloody & complained verry much, I refreshed them with a little grog."

Shortly after leaving the portage and going back into the river for transportation, the explorers entered the Rocky Mountains and the leaders had long since abandoned an earlier plan of sending part of the group back downriver to St. Louis that year. They were running late, they had not met up with the Shoshoni Indians to buy horses, and there was no guarantee that the Indians they met would be friendly. So they drove themselves, eight canoes strong now, making as much as twenty miles a day on the swift river. They passed abandoned Indian camps, fought the clouds of mosquitoes that surged upward everywhere, and were continually wet, either from the rain, the morning dew, or the river itself.

Yet they found adequate time to write detailed entries about the flora and fauna noted along the route, often depending on Sacajawea for information on different uses of plants and their edibility.

Western mourning dove *(Zenaidura macroura marginella)*

On July 18 they found a river that they named Dearborn in honor of the Secretary of War but did not realize it was the river the Indians at Fort Mandan had told them was a shortcut through the mountains to the Lolo Pass. And the next day they reached a section of the river that seemed to cut through virtually vertical canyon walls of black granite, which Lewis named "The Gates of the Rocky Mountains." Towing through this area was almost impossible and there were long gaps between places to step ashore. Rowing was the only method of propulsion, even though the current was unusually swift.

Clark had taken a small party and gone on ahead overland in search of routes and, more important, in search of the Shoshonis. A week later, on July 25, Clark and his four men reached the Three Forks of the Missouri. They left a note at the middle (Madison) and western (Jefferson) forks, telling Lewis to wait for them there while they went on upriver. They walked another twenty miles on their battered and aching feet and climbed a low mountain but still saw no sign of the Indians. They struck out eastward away from the rivers, found the Madison River, and then followed it down to meet Lewis and the rest of the party.

When the entire corps was reunited, Clark was very ill and running a high temperature, so Lewis decided to halt at the Three Forks camp for a couple of days and to send out scouting parties. After each party came back from the three rivers, the leaders agreed that only the Jefferson was the proper route to follow what they hoped would be the headwaters of the Columbia River. The others — the Madison and the Gallatin — headed too far south. Sacajawea recognized some of the landmarks in the confusing area, but she did not remember which of the three streams headed toward her homeland. She recognized the campsite near the junction of the Madison and Jefferson Rivers where she had been captured five years earlier, but her usefulness as a guide and diplomat was not yet apparent.

Clark's thirty-fifth birthday, August 1, 1805, was spent in considerable pain. He was still weak from his recent illness and he had badly cut feet and a boil from some kind of insect bite on his ankle as the party moved slowly up the Jefferson. Although Clark was usually the head scout, his illness kept him with the main party and Lewis took a group ahead, the inevitable Drouillard by his side, looking for the Shoshonis. When they reached the fork in the Jefferson, near present-day Twin Bridges, Montana, they turned up the western branch — the Big Hole River — by mistake and soon discovering that it was not the mainstream, they backtracked and followed the other fork, the Beaverhead River.

Western pileated woodpecker *(Dryocopus pileatus picinus)*

Clark's party was having more problems with the river that grew steadily shallower, swifter, and rockier. When they reached the fork, they also followed the wrong stream because, they suspected, a beaver had felled a stick with a note Lewis had left behind. One canoe upset and two others were almost swamped. Whitehouse was badly hurt in the accident, and the party lost twenty pounds of powder and many provisions. The entire party was markedly tired from ascending the river and many of the men were sick, both physically and mentally, from the incredibly arduous journey they had made from the Great Falls. It was definitely one of the expedition's low points.

A few days later, August 8, Sacajawea became excited and said she recognized a local landmark far ahead, Beaverhead Rock, which today is fourteen miles north of Dillon, Montana. She told the party it was near the summer camp of her people and from there she could lead them up the Lemhi River to the camp and over a low pass to her home country.

Lewis felt that success was finally within his grasp, and he appointed Drouillard, Shields, and McNeal to accompany him in search of the Shoshonis. Instead of their carrying a supply of food, he loaded their packs with one blanket apiece and their weapons, the rest of the space being filled with trade goods. One suspects that at that moment he and Clark would have traded anything — or anyone — to the Indians for the much needed horses.

They found an Indian trail beside the stream and followed it past some high cliffs, which Lewis named Rattlesnake Cliffs for obvious reasons and while they waited and rested, Lewis sent Drouillard out to shoot a deer for lunch. Sending Drouillard out after game was equivalent to sending someone to the grocery store today because he was by far the best hunter of the entire party and probably the most dependable member, other than the leaders themselves.

Almost casually Lewis wrote, "he arrived in about an hour and a half or at noon with three deer skins and the flesh of one of the best of them; we cooked and eat a haisty meal and departed . . ." In other words, Drouillard decided to do a little comparison shopping while he was out.

On August 11, Lewis finally spotted an Indian. They had lost the trail:

> I now sent Drewyer to keep near the creek to my right and

Shields to my left, with orders to surch for the road which
if they found they were to notify me by placing a hat in the
muzzle of their gun. I kept McNeal with me; after having
marched in this order for about five miles I discovered an
Indian on horse back about two miles distant coming down
the plain towards us. with my glass I discovered from his
dress that he was of a different nation than we had yet
seen, and was satisfyed of his being a Sosone; his arms
were a bow and quiver of arrows, and was mounted on an
eligant horse without a saddle, and a small string was
attached to the under jaw of the horse which answered as
a bridle. I was overjoyed at the sight of this stranger and
had no doubt of obtaining a friendly introduction to his
nation provided I could get near enough to him to convince
him of our being whitemen. I therefore proceeded towards
him at my usual pace. when I had arrived within about a
mile he made a halt which I did also and unloosing my
blanket from my pack, I made him the signal of friendship
known to the Indians of the Rocky mountains and those of
the Missouri, which is by holding the mantle or robe in
your hands at two corners and then throwing (it) up in the
air higher than the head bringing it to the earth as if in the
act of spreading it, thus repeating three times . . . this
signal had not the desired effect, he still kept his position
and seemed to view Drewyer and Shields who were now
coming in sight on either hand with an air of suspicion, I
would willingly have made them halt but they were too far
distant to hear me and I feared to make any signal to them
least it should increase the suspicion in the mind of the
Indian of our having some unfriendly design upon him. I
therefore haistened to take out of my sack some beads a
looking glas and a few trinkets which I had brought with
me for this purpose and leaving my gun and pouch with
McNeal advanced unarmed towards him. he remained in
the same stedfast poisture untill I arrived in about 200
paces of him when he turned his horse about and began to
move off slowly from me; I now called to him in as loud a
voice as I could command repeating the word *tab-ba-
bone,* which in their language signifyes *white-man.* but
looking over his sholder he still kept his eye on Drewyer
and Shields who wer still advancing neither of them haveing segacity enough to recollect the impropriety of advanc-

ing when they saw me thus in parley with the Indian. I now made a signal to these men to halt, Drewyer obeyed but Shields who afterwards told me that he did not observe the signal still kept on   the Indian halted again and turned his horse about as if to wait for me, and I beleive would have remained untill I came up whith him had it not been for Shields who still pressed forward. when I arrived within about 150 paces I again repepeated the word tab-ba-bone and held up the trinkits in my hands and striped up my shirt sleve to give him an opportunity of seeing the colour of my skin and advanced leasurely towards him but he did not remain untill I got nearer than about 100 paces when he suddonly turned his horse about, gave him the whip leaped the creek and disapeared in the willow bush in an instant and with him vanished all my hopes of obtaining horses for the present. I now called the men to me and could not forbare abraiding them a little for their want of attention and imprudence on this occasion.

The last remark is probably the understatement of this particular journal entry.

They stopped to cook breakfast near the creek, and Lewis assembled a peace offering of moccasin awls, several strands of beads, paint, and a looking glass and attached the bag on a pole driven into the ground near the fire. They were drenched by a thunderstorm and hailstones, and the rain washed away the tracks of the lone horseman. They prowled the valley a bit more and found evidence that the Indians had been digging for roots in the area and they saw fresh hoofprints of eight or ten horses.

The next day they continued their search for the Indians, walking back and forth across the valley in search of any Indian road or trail they could find to follow. They found a trail at last that followed a small stream to the west, which they gave the practical name of Trail Creek, and McNeal at one point straddled it and said that he thanked God he had lived "to bestride the mighty & heretofore deemed endless Missouri." Unfortunately, his joy was misplaced because they were not at the true headwaters: the ultimate source actually is at Red Rock Lake in the corner of Montana near Yellowstone National Park, but he went through life believing he was the first to straddle the Missouri River, and he earned the premature accolade. They continued on, crossed Lemhi Pass to the Pacific drainage, and camped on the western slope.

The next morning they continued along the trail and after traveling about four miles across the valley floor, they saw an Indian with two squaws and a few dogs. The Indians saw Lewis and his men and after looking at the white men a few minutes, two of them sat down as if to wait for their arrival. When they were about a half mile away, Lewis left his pack and rifle behind and unfurled the American flag and they began walking single-file toward the Indians. The women took off over a hill and the man stayed until they were about a hundred yards away, then he, too "absconded. tho' I frequently repeated the word *tab-ba-bone* sufficiently loud for him to have heard it. I now haistened to the top of the hill where they had stood but could see nothing of them. the dogs were less shye than their masters

they came about me pretty close. I therefore thought of tying a handkerchief about one of their necks with some beads and other trinkets and then let them loose to surch their fugitive owners thinking by this means to convince them of our pacific disposition towards them but the dogs would not suffer me to take hold of them; they also soon disappeared."

Some linguists have suggested that the words Lewis learned from Sacajawea — tab-ba-bone — might have been the root of the problem in making early contact with the Shoshoni. Sacajawea had been asked for the proper word, the linguists say, and she gave them the closest, which actually meant "stranger" or "outsider" since they had no word for white man for the very good reason they had never seen one. Perhaps the Shoshoni thought it both strange and ominous that these strange men repeated the obvious over and over. Their sense of self-preservation being much more highly developed than their curiosity, they simply vacated the premises.

Lewis stubbornly kept on the trail, hoping eventually to find the large encampment of Indians, and he wasn't unaware of the danger he might face because he had told Clark to "carry on" should he become permanently absent from the expedition.

After another mile the trail was well used and dusty and Lewis suddenly came on a native woman and two young girls just beyond a ravine that had kept them from seeing each other sooner. One of the girls immediately took to her heels, but the other two stood their ground and watched as Lewis went through his set routine of putting aside his armory and taking up his blanket, gifts, and one-word vocabulary. The woman and girl were frightened and sat down as if expecting to be killed. Lewis took the woman by her arm, raised her to her feet, showed her the white skin beneath his sleeve, repeated the word tab-ba-bone for perhaps the thousandth time during the past few days, and apparently convinced her he intended no harm. Then Drouillard, McNeal, and Shields walked up and joined them.

Lewis asked Drouillard to use sign language to the old woman and have her call the other girl back before she ran off to warn the whole village and keep them from swooping down on them in anger. The old woman persuaded the girl to come back fortunately, and Lewis distributed gifts among them and even painted the cheeks of all three with vermilion. Then, everyone being pleased with the turn of events, they all strolled down the trail toward the camp.

After walking two miles, a band of about sixty braves came in at a hard gallop. Lewis walked on ahead of the others to meet them and watched as the chief and two others spoke to the women to find out who the white men were and what gifts they had given.

A Shoshoni tepee

"These men then advanced and embraced me very affectionately in their way which is by puting their left arm over your wright sholder clasping your back, while they apply their left cheek to yours and frequently vociferate the word *ah-hi-e, ah-hi-e* that is, I am much pleased, I am much rejoiced. bothe parties now advanced and we wer all carresed and besmeared with their grease and paint till I was heartily tired of the national hug."

Lewis stoked up a pipe and it was passed all around; he then presented the chief with a flag and other trinkets. The Indians returned the favor by painting the four visitors. Then they walked about four miles north through the valley to the Indian camp, where the white men were made comfortable in a skin tipi, the only one in the village.

They had not eaten since the previous evening and when the chief gave them some dried cakes of serviceberries and chokeberries, they wolfed them down. Later that evening another Indian offered Lewis a "small morsel of the flesh of an antelope boiled, and a peice of fresh salmon roasted; both of which I eat with a very good relish. this was the first salmon I had seen and perfectly convinced me that we were on the waters of the Pacific Ocean.''

The next day Lewis went out and looked over the herd of horses owned by the Indians, which numbered around 700 head. He was impressed with them and said they would ''make a figure on the South side of James River or the land of fine horses.'' Some of the horses carried Spanish brands and about twenty head of mules were included in the herd, which the Indians prized highly.

Lewis held another council with the chief, Cameahwait, with Drouillard translating the sign language easily and swiftly. Lewis wanted to borrow some horses and return to pick up Clark and the remainder of the party. But Cameahwait was afraid to go because the Blackfeet often raided them, had done so earlier that summer, and had killed or captured twenty men and several horses, and destroyed all the tipis except the one Lewis had slept in. After trying everything else, Lewis finally challenged the chief's personal bravery and finally convinced him to go with them back over Lemhi Pass to pick up Clark and the others.

In the meantime, Clark's party was progressing slowly up the Beaverhead River valley, and Clark took Sacajawea with him and walked on ahead. On the same morning that Lewis and the Indians recrossed Lemhi Pass and went looking for Clark, Sacajawea had seen an Indian she knew. Clark saw her stop, dance with joy, wave to him, and point toward some mounted Indians approaching. She made signs to Clark that they were from her nation by sucking her fingers to show this was the land where she was suckled as a child.

Lewis was very concerned when he arrived at the appointed meeting place to find that Clark wasn't there as he had expected him to be. Clark had shown a bit of uncharacteristic stubbornness along the way by refusing to leave the boats behind, as he probably should have, because the stream was so shallow the boats had to be dragged.

When they were reunited on August 17, they decided on the name for the camp — Camp Fortunate — because it was where they had first seen Indians, which meant that they still stood a chance of reaching the Pacific before winter. But first they had to bargain for horses and then find someone to lead them through the mountains to navigable water.

But that great day of August 17 was an important one for another member of the party. First, Sacajawea saw a young Indian woman she knew and ran to embrace her. She had been captured by the Minitaris at the same time as Sacajawea, and they immediately recognized each other. Later in the day, Sacajawea was called into the council with Cameahwait to help interpret and as she was getting ready to sit down, she recognized the chief as her brother. She leaped up and embraced him, then threw her blanket over him and wept uncontrollably. She regained a measure of self-control after a few minutes and served as interpreter from Shoshoni to Minitari. Charbonneau translated into French and Labiche finally brought everything together in English.

Lewis and Clark made some strong promises to the Shoshonis, including one that the government would help to protect them against their enemies and establish trading posts for them. In return they expected the use of horses and guide service through the Bitterroot Mountains and down the Pacific Slope to the sea. The Shoshoni chief agreed without undue haggling.

A party of hunters went out that day and brought back three deer and an antelope "which was eaten in a Short time," Clark wrote, "the Indians being so harrassed & compelled to move about in those rugid mountains that they are half Starved liveing at this time on berries & roots which they geather in the plains. Those people are not begerly but generous, only one has asked me for anything and he for powder."

The next day, August 18, was Lewis's thirty-first birthday, and he was less than enthusiastic about his position in the universe and displayed the same sort of melancholia many men of accomplishment fall heir to:

"This day I completed my thirty first year, and conceived that I had in all human probability now existed about half the period which I am to remain in the Sublunary world. I reflected that I had as yet done but little, or to advance the information of the succeeding generation. I viewed with regret the many hours I have spent in indolence, and now soarly feel the want of that information which those hours would have given me had they been judiciously expended. but since they are past and cannot be recalled, I dash from me the gloomy thought, and resolved in future, to redouble my exertions and at least indeavour to promote those two primary objects of human existence, by giving them the aid of that portion of talents which nature and fortune have bestoed on me; or in future, to live *for mankind,* as I have heretofore lived *for myself.*"

True to his word, Lewis was back on duty the next day observing and reporting with a keen eye. His reports on the Indians and their culture could well serve as models for anthropology students. His writings are notable for their lack of judgment according to his moral standards, and both he and Clark appeared ready to accept the Indians for what they were rather than what later missionaries and bureaucrats thought they should be.

"they have more children among them than I expected to have seen among a people who procure subsistence with such difficulty. there are but few old persons, nor did they appear to treat those with much tenderness or rispect. The man is the sole proprytor of his wives and daughters, and can barter or dispose of either as he thinks proper. a plurality of wives is common among them, but these are not generally sisters as with the Minnitares & Mandans but are purchased of different fathers. The father frequently disposes of his infant daughters in marriage to men who are grown or to men who have sons for whom they think proper to provide wives. the compensation given in such cases usually consists of horses or mules which the father receives at the time of contract and converts to his own uce. the girl remains with her parents untill she is conceived to have obtained the age of puberty which with them is considered to be about the age of 13 or 14 years. the female at this age is surrendered to her soveriegn lord and husband agreeably to contract, and with her is frequently restored by the father quite as much as he received in the first instance payment for his daughter; but this is discretionary with the father. Sah-car-gar-we-ah (Sacajawea) had been thus disposed of before she was taken by the Minnetares, or had arrived to the years of puberty. the husband was yet living with this band. he was more than double her age and had two other wives. he claimed her as his wife but said that as she had had a child by another man, who was Charbono, that he did not want her. They seldom correct their children particularly the boys who soon become masters of their own acts. they give as a reason that it cows and breaks the sperit of the boy to whip him, and that he never recovers his independence of mind after he is grown. They treat their women but with little rispect, and compel them to perform every species of drudgery."

Although they had had no previous contact with white men, Lewis found that the Indians suffered from venereal diseases, and that they usually died from this condition. "this seems strong proof that these disorders bothe ganaraehah and Louis [lues] Venerae are native disorders of America, tho' these people have suffered much by the small pox which is known to be imported . . ." Others have since agreed with Lewis that gonorrhea and syphilis cannot be blamed on the white man since there is ample evidence that it existed, at least in mild form, all across the North American continent prior to 1492.

The Shoshoni seemed to spend almost equal time searching for food and fleeing the hostile tribes that came up the Missouri River valley each summer. They told Lewis that "from the middle of May to the first of September these people reside on the waters of the Columbia where they consider themselves in perfect security from their enimies as they have not as yet ever found their way to this retreat; during this season the salmon furnish the principal part of their subsistence and as this fish either perishes or returns about the 1st of September they are compelled at this season in surch of subsistence to resort to the Missouri, in the vallies of which, there is more game even within the mountains. here they move slowly down the river in order to

Shira's moose *(Alces alces shirasi)*

collect and join other bands either of their own nation or the Flatheads, and having become sufficiently strong as they conceive venture on the Eastern side of the Rockey mountains into the plains, where the buffaloe abound. but they never leave the interior of the mountains while they can obtain a scanty subsistence, and always return as soon as they have acquired a good stock of dryed meat in the plains; when this stock is consumed they venture again into the plains; thus alternately obtaining their food at the risk of their lives and retiring to the mountains, while they consume it. These people are now on the eve of their departure for the Missouri, and inform us that they expect to be joined at or about the three forks by several bands of their own nation, and a band of the Flatheads.''

At Lewis' urging the Indians gave him what information they possessed on the western slope of the mountains; he wasn't especially happy with it because it meant the trip down to sea level, and into the Columbia River, was much rougher than the group had expected. The chiefs told them that the Lemhi River flowed into a larger river, the Salmon, which was filled with rapids beneath steep cliffs that would not permit them to line their boats through from the bank. Also, game was scarce along the river, they said, and the trees were too small for building canoes. Instead, the expedition should go farther north and catch a trail that the Nez Percés used to cross the Bitterroots each year, although they warned that game was equally scarce there, too, and the Nez Percé usually went without sufficient food while making the crossing.

The captains decided to risk the trail, which led over Lolo Pass, and Clark went ahead with a group of eleven men (including, of course, Drouillard), several Indians, and two of the three horses they had bought from the Indians. Cameahwait himself accompanied Clark in the advance party to help with the purchase of more horses in the Bitterroot Valley, and they were able to obtain the services of a guide of dubious value whom they nicknamed Old Toby.

As usual, Drouillard was out hunting and trapping beaver most of the time, and on Thursday, August 22, he returned to camp not only with a fawn he had killed, but also with, as Lewis dryly remarked, ''a considerable quantity of Indian plunder.'' Drouillard told Lewis that while he was out hunting on horseback, he came on an Indian camp with a young man, an old man, a boy, and three women. He rode up and dismounted, turning his horse out to graze. After about twenty minutes of conversation, the women went out and collected all their horses and saddled them up. Drouillard decided to leave and continue his hunt but made one of his very few errors of judgment: he left his gun behind while he walked over to get his mount.

"the Indians perceiving him at the distance of fity paces immediately mounted their horses, the young man took the gun, and the whole of them left their baggage and laid whip to their horses directing their course to the pass of the mountains. finding himself deprived of his gun he immediately mounted his horse and pursued; after runing them about 10 miles the horses of two of the women nearly gave out and the young fellow with the gun from their frequent crys slackened his pace and being on a very fleet horse road around the women at a little distance   at length Drewyer overtook the women and by signs convinced them that he did not wish to hirt them   they then halted and the young fellow approached still nearer, he asked him for his gun but the only part of the answer which he could understand was pahkee which he knew to be the name by which they called their enimies, watching his opportunity when the fellow was off his guard he suddonly rode along side of him seized his gun and wrested her out of his hands. the young fellow finding Drewyer too strong for him and discovering that he must yeald the gun had presents of mind to open the pan and cast [out] the priming before he let the gun escape his hands;   now finding himself devested of the gun he turned his horse about and laid whip leaving the women to follow him as well as they could. Drewyer now returned to the place they had left their baggage and brought it with him to my camp. it consisted of several dressed and undressed skins; a couple of bags woven . . . of the bark of the silk-grass, each containing about a bushel of dried service burries some chokeberry cakes and about a bushel of roots of three different kinds dried and prepared for uce which were foalded in as many parchment hides of buffaloe. some flint and the instrument of bone for manufactureing the flint into arrow points."

In spite of his carelessness, Drouillard seemed to have come out of the situation well ahead of the competition.

Lewis also arranged for the purchase of six more horses, paying the equivalent of six dollars each in merchandise, and he commented on the honesty of the Indians, saying that they did not "crowd" their camp, and when they borrowed an article, they always returned it. The tribes they were to meet a few weeks later along the Columbia were quite another story.

Clark and his group moved on northward about fifty miles, scouting the Lemhi and eventually the Salmon to see if the information the Indians had given them was correct. After climbing around the ragged mountains and watching the whitewater of the Salmon, the famous "River of No Return," Clark decided the Indians were indeed telling the truth and headed back to meet the rest of the party. In the meantime, Clark had named the Salmon Lewis' River.

Clark sent John Colter back on a horse with a message of his findings to Lewis and the rest of the party and encouraged Lewis to buy as many horses as he could for the trip over Lolo Pass. He was very firm in his assessment of the Salmon River, and it has since been pointed out that they found perhaps the roughest part of the entire Rocky Mountains — not the highest, but the roughest.

In spite of the need for haste and the long hours spent in the formalities of bargaining for the mounts, both leaders found time to comment on the wildlife around them, and Clark was the first to note the existence of the passenger pigeon west of the Continental Divide. It was while Clark was out on this exploratory trip that he also found "a Bird of the woodpecker kind which fed on Pine burs   its Bill and tale white the wings black every other part of a light brown, and about the size of a robin." This was the *Nucifraga columbiana,* more commonly known as Clark's nutcracker. It was Clark's turn to have a bird named for him because, even though they had no way of knowing they would one day be so honored, a bird Lewis had described a month earlier near Helena, Montana ("I saw a black woodpecker [or crow] today about the size of the lark woodpecker as black as a crow"), was later named *Asyundesmus lewis,* Lewis' woodpecker.

They also noted the Shoshoni wore some kind of sheepskin that the Indians said came from a sheep about the size of a common domesticated sheep which they found in the high mountains. Clark saw one at a distance, but neither he nor Lewis were able to approach sufficiently close to describe one in detail. This, of course, was the Rocky Mountain goat (*Oreamnos americanus americanus*), and their mention of it was the first written reference.

About the time they crossed a gap in the mountains that is

Mountain goat

today called Lost Trail Pass, Lewis, for some unknown reason, made virtually no entries in his journal until January 1, 1806. Whether he did not make entries or he made them and they were lost is not known. Clark made up for lost time during the next four months, and the entries, with inventive spelling and punctuation, still amuse and puzzle readers.

The trip from the Lemhi to the entrance to Lolo Pass was one of the roughest pieces of terrain along the Montana-Idaho border, and Gass, not one to mince words in his brief journal, called it the "worst road (if road it can be called) that was ever traveled." The pack horses frequently lost their footing, sometimes toppling over backward with the heavy load, and it was here in one spill that Lewis's last thermometer was broken. The group ran short of food and snow fell as they reached the higher elevations. They tried living on berries but finally had to dig into their larder and consume the last of their pork. Finally, four of the Indians gave up and turned back, leaving only Old Toby and his son.

Six days after they left the Shoshoni behind, they finally emerged onto a mile-wide valley where they found an abundance of roots and herbs to alleviate their hunger. It was in this valley, now called Ross's Hole, that they met a band of about 400 Indians whom Lewis and Clark, for reasons known to them, called the Flatheads. As the great Lewis and Clark scholar, Paul

Flathead profile

Russell Cutright, wrote: "These Indians no more had flat heads than the Blackfeet had black feet or the Gros Ventres uniformly had big bellies. However, the name Lewis and Clark applied to them has stuck with them since." The Indians told the explorers they were Ootlashoots of the Tushepau nation, who were in the Salishan linguistic family of the Pacific Northwest.

Lewis and Clark immediately began bargaining with them for horses, and Clark later explained that they conversed in this round-robin manner: "Our convn. with the Tushepaws was held thro' a boy whom we found among them . . . I spoke in English to Labieche . . . he translated it to Chaboneau in French . . . he to his wife in Minnetaree . . . she in Shoshone to the boy . . . the boy in Tushepaw to that nation." In spite of this handicap, they were able to buy eleven horses and traded seven of their own that were badly galled from the packsaddles.

Three days later they arrived at what is known as Travelers Rest, a broad prairie near the mountains where the Lolo Creek enters Bitterroot River. It was here that they would turn directly west and follow the small stream to and beyond its source over Lolo Pass. They decided to rest there a day and devote part of it to exploring the general area, and a group followed the Bitterroot River about ten miles to present-day Missoula, Montana, where the Bitterroot joins the Blackfoot River.

It was also at Travelers Rest that the party received a bit of depressing intelligence. Back at Mandan they had been told of a shortcut to the site at which they were now camped by following a feeder stream due west. It was a rather complicated route that would have involved the services of a guide and a string of pack horses, but it would have taken them four days rather than the fifty-three days necessary to reach Travelers Rest. Also, they were told to explore the Missouri to its source and seek a route across the mountains. Clark accepted the information calmly and without comment, but they put the route to use the following summer when Lewis headed north from Travelers Rest into Blackfeet country.

Now the explorers were in for the second punishing portage, one almost as dangerous as that around the Great Falls and one from which they wondered at times if they would emerge alive. Although Indians had told them the trip over Lolo Pass was a five-day journey, they were not certain the estimate was accurate, especially after having had a taste of the Bitterroots between the Shoshoni village and Travelers Rest. In fact, it was an eleven-day trip and their closest brush with starvation.

5

Bitterroots to the Pacific

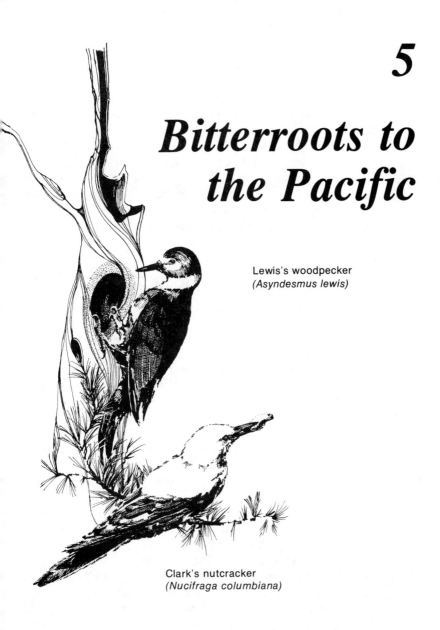

Lewis's woodpecker
(Asyndesmus lewis)

Clark's nutcracker
(Nucifraga columbiana)

The group set out late in the afternoon of September 11, 1805 for Lolo Pass, after being delayed while searching for two lost horses. Clark wrote that they sent out four of their best hunters in advance "as usial" and went up a narrow valley about seven miles and camped at some old Indian lodges. As if a portent, the hunters brought no game to camp that night.

Rocky Mountain
maple seed *(Acer
glabrum)*

They woke to a "white frost" the next morning and rode past an old Indian sweat house, similar to a sauna, then left the good trail behind. They began to find fallen timber across their route, together with almost impenetrable brush and steep, dangerous sidehills. The hunters brought only one pheasant* to the pot that night.

The third day Lewis and four men stayed behind to hunt for Lewis' and a guide's mounts, which had strayed during the night. During the day they stopped at what is now Lolo Hot Springs, which "spouted" from the rocks. Then Old Toby took a wrong turn in the trail and they went about three miles out of their way. After they returned to the trail, Clark called for a halt to let the men rest and the horses graze while they waited for Lewis and the other guide. They crossed Lolo Pass that afternoon and camped that night about two miles down the Pacific Slope. The hunters brought in a deer and some pheasants, not much of a meal for about forty people, but better than the fare of the previous two nights.

The next day opened with snow on the mountains and rain and hail in the valleys. The group criss-crossed the stream they called Glade Creek, but which today is called Packer Creek, and found an abandoned Indian camp with a weir in the stream to catch fish. Unfortunately it was not assembled and it held no bounty. They camped that night opposite a small island where a stream enters the river, and they named the site Colt-killed Creek for the very good reason that they killed a colt for dinner. From this spot westward the tributary today is known as the Lochsa, and it joins the Clearwater River a few miles downstream.

They left early the following day, which was overcast, and traveled over increasingly difficult terrain, leaving the river for higher elevations and making extremely steep climbs while doing so. "Several horses Sliped and roled down Steep hills which hurt them verry much   the one which Carried my desk & Small trunk Turned over & roled down a mountain for 40 yards & lodged against a tree, broke the Desk   the horse escaped and appeared but little hurt   Some other verry much hurt!" Two of their horses gave out on them and were too hurt to continue, so they left them behind. They killed nothing except two pheasant

---

*The word "pheasant" is used in this chapter as Lewis and Clark used it in their journals. They mistakenly referred to grouse as pheasants. The latter were not introduced into the American West until the 1890s.

that day and when they made camp that night, they melted snow to drink and cooked some more horseflesh.

On September 16 it began to snow about three hours before dawn and continued all day. When they started out, the snow was four inches deep; by nightfall it was six to eight inches deep. Clark walked ahead to break trail and often lost it, sometimes wandering back and forth in front of the miserable procession several minutes before finding the trail again. "I have been wet and as cold in every part as I ever was in my life, indeed I was at one time fearfull my feet would freeze in the thin Mockirsons which I wore, after a Short Delay in the middle of the Day, I took one man and proceeded on as fast as I could about six miles to a Small branch passing to the right, halted and built fires for the party against their arrival which was at Dusk, verry cold and much fatigued. . . . Killed a Second Colt which we all Suped hartily on and thought it fine meat." During the day he saw four black-tailed deer and his gun misfired seven times because, as he found out after it was too late, the flint was loose. "to describe the road of this day would be a repitition of yesterday except the Snow which made it much worse." He noted that often during the day they had kept on the trail by finding trees that had been rubbed by packs on Indian horses.

They had other problems the next day. Several horses had broken loose, and they weren't able to get under way until about one o'clock that afternoon. Snow continued falling both from the sky and from tree branches, then down their necks. They kept to the high ground in the snow because the going was easier than down in the valley where no snow had accumulated. They killed a few pheasant, which was vastly insufficient for meals, "which compelled us to kill Something, a Coalt being the most useless part of our Stock he fell a Prey to our appetites. The horses fell & hurt themselves very much."

On the eighth day, September 18, Clark took six hunters with him and rode ahead in search of deer and "passed over a countrey Similar to the one of yesterday   more fallen timber   passed Several runs & Springs passing to the right . . . made 32 miles and Encamped on a bold running Creek passing to the left which I call *Hungery* Creek as at that place we had nothing to eate. Drewyer shot at a Deer we did not get it. Killed nothing in those emence mountains of stones falling timber & brush."

The following morning they found a stray horse. "I derected

Salmonberry
(Rubus spectabilis)

Camas *(Camassia quamash)*

him killed and hung up for the party after takeing a brackfast off for our Selves which we thought fine.'' They followed Hungry Creek eight miles, then found Collins Creek and camped that night on what is now Lolo Creek. ''I killed 2 Pheasents, but few birds . . . as we decend the mountain the heat becomes more proseptable every mile.''

On the tenth day they broke out of the timber and onto a broad, grassy plain and ''proceeded on through a butifull Countrey for three miles to a Small Plain in which I found maney Indian lodges, at the distance of 1 mile from the lodges I met 3 (Indian) boys, when they saw me (they) ran and hid themselves, (in the grass) (I desmounted and gave my gun and horse to one of the men) searched (in the grass) found (2 of the boys) gave them Small pieces of ribin & Sent them forward to the village   (Soon after) a man Came out to meet me . . .'' The Indian took them to a large lodge which he said belonged to a chief who was gone to fight a battle off to the southwest and who would be back in to or three weeks.

There were several women in the camp and they gave Lewis and his men pieces of buffalo, dried salmonberries, and camas roots, the first time they had tasted the latter, a staple of the Indians' diet from the Bitterroots to the Cascades. The Indians were Nez Percé and Clark said they were ''large Portley men Small women & handsom featured.'' That night he found himself ''verry unwell . . . from eateing the fish and roots too freely.''

The next morning Clark stayed in camp with the Indians and sent the six men out hunting, and they again returned empty-handed. But they collected ''a horse load of roots & 3 Sammon & sent R Fields with one Indian to meet Capt. Lewis,'' then set out with the other men down toward the Clearwater River, where a principal chief, Twisted Hair, was fishing. They arrived late that night, about 11 P.M. and Clark found him ''a Chearfull man with apparant siencerity.'' He gave Twisted Hair one of the medals especially struck for the expedition, sat up smoking and conversing by sign language until about 1 A.M. and went to bed. Clark's last entry for that day's journal was succinct: ''I am verry sick to day and puke which relive me.''

The next morning the party went down the river about a mile and a half and found Twisted Hair's camp on an island. The chief paddled over in a canoe and took Clark to his camp. Then he left a man there to watch their baggage and immediately turned back to meet Lewis and the rest of the party, taking with

Balsam root *(Buphthalmum sagittatum)*

him three deer that Shields had killed. "I took a small pice & changed for his horse which was fresh & proced on   this horse threw me 3 times which hurt me some.   at Dark met Capt. Lewis Encamped at the first Village   men much fatigued & reduced, much rejoiced to find something to eate of which they appeared to partake plentifully." Perhaps remembering the previous night's gastronomical disturbances, Clark said he "cautioned them of the Consequences of eateing too much &etc."

Lewis' crossing had been rougher because he had a larger party and more pack animals to contend with. Although he did not keep a journal during this period, he apparently worked later from Clark's daily account, and between them the two leaders compiled a complete picture not only of this part of the adventure but of other parts as well. Apparently Lewis made field notes as he went along, because while they were on the verge of starvation, he made frequent and detailed references to the wildlife along the Lolo Trail. Also, for the first and probably only time on the journey, they broke into Lewis' 193 pounds of "portable soup," which from all accounts was dreadful stuff. As hungry as everyone was, it was almost worse than having nothing.

Yet Lewis stuck to his job and in the process found and described on September 20, "a species of bird which I had never seen before. It was reather larger than a robin, tho' much it's

Bitterroot
*(Lewisia
rediviva)*

101

form and action. the colours were a blueish brown on the back the wings and tale black, as wass a strip above the croop ¾ of an inch wide in front of the nect, and two others of the same colour passed from its eyes back along the sides of the head. the top of the head, neck brest and belley and butts of the wing were of a fine yellowish brick reed. it was feeding on the buries of a species of showmake or ash which grows common in (this) country & which I first observed on 2nd of this month.''

Lewis had discovered the black-headed jay *(Cyanocitta stelleri annectens)*, a subspecies of the Steller's jay. Also during his crossing, he killed a few pheasants and a wolf and sent men to catch small crayfish from the streams. But gradually they obtained meat along the route, and the provender sent back or hung in trees by Clark always seemed to arrive just before someone fell in his tracks from starvation.

Once they were all together again in the Nez Percé camp, they began to obtain information on the river below them and found that the river they were on, the Clearwater, soon joined the Snake "2 Sleeps" away and that five sleeps farther on the Snake emptied into the Columbia, and still another five sleeps they would find the first set of falls on the Columbia.

They spent the following day trading with Indians and obtained dried roots, hawthorne berries, fish, and a few other items. They left several gifts with the Indians, including medals, flags, handkerchiefs, knives, and tobacco. Some of the articles were left to be given to the main chief when he returned from his war, wherever that was. Clark referred to the war so casually that the chief might as well have been away trading for horses.

The next day they rounded up all their horses and went back down the Clearwater to Twisted Hair's island camp; nearly the entire crew was ill, apparently from having food in their bellies again. "Several men So unwell that they were Compelled to lie on the Side of the road for Some time others obliged to be put on horses,'' and Lewis himself was barcly able to ride on a "jentle horse which was furnished by the Chief.'' Clark doctored them with "rushes Pills,'' the contents of which were known only by Dr. Benjamin Rush of Philadelphia, who was referred to Lewis by Jefferson. It is on record that Lewis spent $90.69 for medicine before leaving on the expedition.

Apparently the main cause of their illness, which lasted for several days, was not so much the quality or quantity, as it was the variety, of the food. The men had been accustomed to eating red meat from the buffalo, horse, dog, and wolf, and now their diet was suddenly changed to roots and salmon.

On September 24 Clark and Twisted Hair went downriver in search of timber large enough to build canoes. They landed just below the place where the North Fork of the Clearwater enters and set up a canoe-building camp near what is today Orofino, Idaho. They felled five large ponderosa pines, and those who were able to work began hewing out the canoes and for the first time adopted the Indian method of burning out the logs. This was done primarily because many of the men were still sick or weak; on September 27, when all else failed to cure them, Clark sent John Colter out and he brought back a deer. With this addition to the diet and a few more such trips by Colter and by Drouillard when *he* recovered — by October 4 Clark wrote that Lewis was recovering and that others had already returned to full duty. Clark, too, was sick about four days but did not hold up the procession when they launched the canoes.

Finally, on October 7, they were ready to get under way again. They had become very friendly with the Nez Percé and were later to speak of them more highly than of other tribes, including the Shoshoni. They had made arrangements with Twisted Hair to watch their horses during their absence, and they marked their thirty eight horses by braiding their manes in a particular way.

If the Bitterroot passage was the toughest part of the trip, then the trip down the Clearwater, the Snake, and finally the Columbia Rivers held the best possibilities for immediate disaster. Previously, all their river experience had been against the current, all the way from St. Louis to their meeting with the Shoshoni. Now they were going down a series of rivers, each with its sets of rapids and each swifter than most of the Missouri.

Ponderosa pine
(Pinus ponderosa)

They immediately had trouble navigating the rapids and punched holes in some of the canoes the first day out. On the second day Sgt. Gass's canoe was first nearly turned over, then sprung a leak, and sunk in some rapids. "the men, Several of which Could not Swim hung on to the Canoe, I had one of the other Canoes unloaded & with the assistance of our Small Canoe and one Indian Canoe took out everything & toed the empty Canoe on Shore, one man Thompson a little hurt, everything wet particularly the greater part of our Small Stock of Merchandize, had everything opened, and two Sentinels put over them to keep off the Indians, who are enclined to theave haveing Stole Several Small articles those people appeared disposed to give us every assistance in their power during our distress.''

At one of these Snake Indian camps, they found two chiefs who said they would accompany them, acting as guides. They replaced Old Toby and his son, who left without receiving their pay. They took two horses and were never seen again. It was also that day an Indian woman, as Gass put it, ''took a crazy fit, and cut her arms from the wrists to the shoulders, with flint.'' Clark seemed to think she had only ''fain'd madness &c.&c.''

From the confluence of the Clearwater and Snake, the party was within sight of Indians nearly all the way through the Cascade Mountains to the Pacific. The journals of Lewis and Clark take on more of an anthropological tone at this point than the recounting of an adventure, although the rivers certainly gave them enough of the latter. And they were now out of the pine woods of Idaho and into the treeless rolling plains of eastern Washington, covered with bunchgrass. It was a hostile land for man then, and a few years later the artist Paul Kane nearly starved to death traversing the Great Columbia Plain from north to south. There were no vast herds of buffalo, antelope, elk, deer, or other wildlife so common on the eastern slope of the continent. The explorers relied mainly on salmon purchased from the Indians along the bank, and they ate an inordinate amount of dogs as they traveled west that fall and east upriver again the following spring and summer.

On October 12 they went through one of the worst sets of rapids on the lower Snake River (fortunately they did not have to face the horrors of Hells Canyon on the Snake, upriver from the Clearwater). They first hit a hard wind that blew cold on their wet clothing, and they heard the rapids ahead of which the Indians had warned them, what later was named the Texas Rapids, near Riparia, Washington, and what has long since been covered by dam backwaters.

''we found (it) long and dangerous about 2 miles in length, and maney turns necessary to Stear Clare of the rocks, which appeared to be in every direction. The Indians went through & our small canoe followed them, as it was late we deturmined to camp above untill the morning''

The rest of the canoes made it through the rapids with no difficulty, and the next day, ''A windey dark raney morning,''

Rapids on the Snake River

they went through other rapids just as bad. Then they passed a river that entered the Snake through a "Chanel of about 20 yards between rugid rocks for the distance of a mile and a half, and a rapid rockey chanel for 2 miles above." They named it Drewyer's River, which name was later changed to the Palouse River. The Palouse, the largest Snake tributary below the Clearwater, was the site of an important archaeological dig where human bones 12,000 years old were found. Then dam backwaters flooded the site.

On October 14 they were about thirty miles below the Palouse when they struck another set of bad rapids, the Pine-tree Rapids, which they wisely stopped to scout.

In decending three Stern Canoes stuck fast for some time on the head of the rapid and one struck a rock in the worst part, fortunately all landed Safe below the rapid which was nearly 3 miles in length. here we dined, and for the first time for three weeks past I had a good dinner of Blue wing Teel, after dinner we Set out and had not proceded on two miles before our Stern Canoe in passing thro a Short rapid opposit the head of an Island, run on a Smothe rock and turned broad Side, the men got out on the (rock) all except one of our Indian Chiefs who swam on Shore, The canoe filed and sunk a number of articles floated out, Such as the mens bedding clothes & skins. the Lodge &c&c.

the greater part of which were cought by 2 of the Canoes, whilst a 3rd was unloading & Steming the Swift current to the relief of the men on the rock, who could with much dificuelty hold the Canoe however in about an hour we got the men and canoe to shore with the Loss of Some bedding Tomahawks shot pouched skins Clothes &c&c. all wet   we had every article exposed to the Sun to dry on the Island, our loss in provisions is verry considerable all our roots was in the canoe that Sunk, and Cannot be dried Sufficient to save, our loose powder was also in the Canoe and is all wete. This I think may be saved,   In this Island we found some Split timber the parts of a house which the Indians had verry securely covered with Stone, we also observed a place where the Indians had burried their fish, we have made it a point at all times not to take any thing belonging to the Indians even their wood.   but this time we are Compelled to violate that rule and take a part of the split timber we find here buried for firewood, as no other is to be found in any direction.

They later were to violate their rule again at Fort Clatsop, with almost humorous results.

The following day was warm and Clark noted that the plain on each side of the river "is wavering" from the heat waves. Lewis climbed to the bank and walked awhile and could see the Cascade Mountains in the distance. They ran some more rapids without much difficulty, and the next day, October 16, they left what they had named the Lewis River and at last entered the Columbia.

They were still in constant sight of Indians and shortly after entering the Columbia, about 200 Indians formed a circle around the party and sung to them for awhile, accompanying themselves on drums. The party bought seven dogs from the Indians and they also received some fish as gifts in return for the shirts, handkerchiefs, and medals Lewis and Clark presented to them. That night the Indians helped them collect fuel, mostly weeds and willow bushes, and one Indian gave Clark about twenty pounds of "verry fat Dried horse meat."

When they began descending the Columbia, they saw salmon by the hundreds of thousands, some still alive and swimming in the clear water, others piled up dead on the banks and in stillwater pools. Clark thumped one on the head as he drifted past and the Indians, following in a canoe, hauled it aboard.

The Indians called the river the "Tarcouche tesse," a name Clark used frequently in the journals.

The explorers cut a wide swath through the dog population along the Columbia. Students of the expedition have counted at least fifty purchases on the downriver trip and perhaps as many on the return voyage. The men didn't mind eating dog and horse meat in the least, but they never learned to adapt completely to a fish diet in spite of the abundance of salmon and steelhead along the river that fall. Part of the problem may have been the result of the Indians' unconcern over the freshness of the fish.

The journals make frequent mention of the lack of fuel for fires along the river from the confluence of the Snake to the Cascades and complain of the great cost of buying firewood from the Indians. By the time the waters of the Columbia reach this area, the river has flowed through more than 200 miles of desert, from the central British Columbia barrens south through eastern Washington, and the supply of driftwood obviously is meager. They had to depend on sagebrush, which emits a distasteful and oily smoke, willows, and weeds.

Hoary sagebrush
(*Artemisia cana*)

Clark wrote that the dress of these Indians differed little from the Snake River and Clearwater River Indians, except for the women:

"those above ware long leather Shirts which (are) highly orinmented with beeds shells &c.&c. and those of the main Columbia river only ware a truss or pece of leather tied around them at their hips and drawn tite between ther legs and fastened before So as barely to hide those parts which are so sacredly hid & secured by our women. Those women are more inclined to Corpulency than any we have yet Seen, with low Stature broad faces, heads flatened and the forward (forehead) compressed so as to form a Streight line from the nose to the Crown of the head. . . ."

He also noted a tendency among these Pacific Northwest plains Indians to eye troubles and correctly guessed it was from the constant reflection of the sun off water and snow in the winter, since that part of Washington and Oregon has as much sunlight the year round as other parts of the Great American desert. They also suffered from bad teeth; sometimes the teeth were ground down even with the gums, and Clark again correctly guessed the erosion was caused by sand and grit mixed with the food. He most likely arrived at this conclusion after eating a few meals with the southwest wind blowing at its steady pace and kicking sand into his own food.

The party camped at the confluence of the two great rivers two days; then on October 18, they set out down the broad Columbia with their provisions of the forty dogs, for which they paid "articles of little value, such as bells, thimbles, knitting pins, brass wire and a few beeds." They met the great chief, Yel-lep-pit (or Yellept) the following day, one of the most famous leaders of the Walla Walla tribe, who wanted the party to linger with them a few days. But winter was too close for comfort and they hurried down toward the Columbia Gorge after promising the chief they would visit longer on the return voyage.

Although the party had a difficult time running the rapids of the Snake, the rapids of the Columbia were quite another matter. This stretch of river, about fifty-five miles long through the Cascade Mountains, was by far the most dangerous part of their nautical adventures. They weren't quite as uncomfortable as they were during the portage of the Great Falls of the Missouri, but they were in much more danger. The rapids were much bigger and swifter and on occasion became falls rather than simply whitewater. This factor, combined with their need to reach the ocean before the onset of winter, led them to take chances they might otherwise have avoided.

They had their first difficulty with the rapids on October 21 when they passed through "with much dificuelty" a bad set near the mouth of John Day's River, which they named Lepages's River. From there they had to wind between huge rocks that littered the river for several miles, and on October 22 they pulled over to the bank and stopped to scout the rapids that were more accurately named Celilo Falls. "Here I beheld an emence body of water compressd in a narrow chanel of about 200 yds in width, fomeing over rocks maney of which presented their tops above the water, when at this place Capt. Lewis joined me haveing delayed on the way to examine a root of which the nativs had been digging great quantities in the bottoms of this River. at about two miles above this river appears to be confined between two high hils below which it is divided by numbers of large rocks, and Small Islands covered with a low groth of timber, and had a rapid as far as the narrows, three Small Islands in the mouth of this River, this River haveing no Indian name that we could find out, except the River on which the Snake Indians live, we think it best to leave the nameing of it untill our return." This was the Deschutes River.

After further scouting the falls, they knew another portage was inevitable. They floated on downriver about two miles, then pulled ashore again on the north side, where most of the Indians camped to avoid the Snake Indians who came up from the south. From there they "walked down accompanied by an old man to view the falls, and the best rout for to make a portage which we Soon discovered was much nearest on the Starb Side, and the distance 1200 yards one third of the way on a rock, about 200 yards over a loose Sand collected in a hollar blown by the winds from the bottoms below which was disagreeable to pass, as it was steep and loose. at the lower part of those rapids we arrived at 5 Large Lodges of nativs drying and prepareing fish for market, they gave us Philburts, and berries to eate. we returned droped down to the head of the rapids and took every article except the Canoes across the portage where I had formed a camp in an ellegable Situation for the protection of our Stores from thieft, which we were more fearfull of, than their arrows."

They spent Wednesday, October 23, on the portage, carrying the gear a distance they estimated at 475 yards, then "we were obliged to let the Canoes down by strong ropes of Elk Skin which we had for this purpose, one Canoe in passing this place got loose by the cords breaking, and was cought by the Indians below."

They finished the portage about 3 P.M. that day, "nearly covered with flees which were so thick amongst the Straw and fish Skins at the upper part of the portage at which place the nativs had been Camped not long since; that every man of the party was obliged to Strip naked dureing the time of takeing over the canoes, that they might have an opportunity of brushing the flees off their legs and bodies."

It was here that Clark reported seeing what he though were sea otters and shot one that he lost in the rapids, but they were actually harbor seals.

The second major obstacle was The Dalles, only a short distance downriver from Celilo Falls. Before they took on that particular set of rapids, the two Indians who had accompanied them from the Clearwater said they wanted to return home because they were afraid for their lives once they entered the realm of the Indians below the rapids. But the leaders persuaded them to remain two nights longer "and we would See the nation below and make a peace between them, they replied they 'were anxious to return and See our horses' we insisted on their staying . . . our views were to detain those Chiefs with us, untill we should pass the next falls, which we were told were very bad, and at no great distance below, that they might inform us of any designs of the nativs, and if possible to bring about a peace between them and the tribes below."

Clark wrote that "the first pitch of this falls (The Dalles) is about 20 feet perpendecular, then passing thro' a narrow chanel for 1 mile to a rapid of about 8 feet tall below which the water has no perceptable fall but verry rapid. It may be proper here to remark that from Some obstruction below, the cause of which we have not yet learned, the water in high fluds (which are in the Spring) rise below these falls nearly to a leavel with the water above the falls; the marks of which can be plainly tracd around the falls." This was caused by confinement of rockslides in the river below, Gass correctly noted in his journal.

At "9 oClock a.m." on October 24, Clark "Set out with the party and proceeded on down a rapid Stream of about 400 yards wide at 2-½ miles the river widened into a large bason to the Starb Side on which there is five Lodges of Indians. here a tremendious black rock Presented itself high and Steep appearing to choke up the river; nor could I See where the water passed further than the current was drawn with great velocity to the Lard. Side of this rock at which place I heard a great roreing."

He landed again to scout this particularly nasty set of rapids, which were called the Short Narrows where the lava flows and rockslides had constricted the river to a forty-five-yard gash with sheer canyon walls that made portaging virtually impossible and "the only danger in passing thro those narrows was the whorls and swills arriseing from the Compression of the water, and which I thought (as also our principal watermen Peter Crusat) by good Stearing we could pass down Safe, accordingly I deturmined to pass through this place notwithstanding the horrid appearance of this agitated gut swelling, boiling & whorling in every direction (which from the top of the rock did not appear as bad as when I was in it); however we passed Safe to the astonishment of all if the Inds. of the last Lodges who viewed us from the top of the rock."

Another set of rapids directly below was too much even for Clark and Cruzatte, so they hauled the canoes to shore and

Western gray squirrel *(Sciurus griseus griseus)*

unloaded all the precious cargo. But they changed their minds and shot those rapids, two canoes at a time in case one capsized.

They stayed over one day to repair the canoes with pitch and sent some hunters out for deer, then laid all their gear out to dry. Some of their goods were ruined from getting wet. That evening they had a big party, with Cruzatte playing the fiddle and York dancing to the delight of all. The hunters had killed four deer and four gray squirrels, and a guard on the riverbank had gigged a salmon, all of which was cooked in a little bear oil. Clark declared the salmon to be "one of the most delisious fish I have ever tasted."

During the night the river rose eight inches, which increase Clark knew was not from the tide because there were still falls to be negotiated. He guessed it was from a strong wind that had been blowing, but more likely it was from a thunderstorm somewhere back in the mountains that swelled a feeder stream. They were still plagued by the fleas they carried with them from above the rapids, and Clark said they were "difficuelt to get rid of, perticulary as the men have not a Change of Clothes to put

111

on, they strip off their Clothes and kill the flees, dureing which time they remain nakid.''

They now were in the heart of the trading zone of the Indians, with the coastal tribes coming upriver to meet the inland tribes to barter for food and clothing. The coastal tribes brought with them many articles of clothing and metal goods they had obtained from the white men trading at the mouth of the Columbia. They saw coats, hats, pots, knives, and other goods that could only have been manufactured by the white man, and they then knew they weren't far from the end of the westward journey.

On October 31, they reached the Cascades of the Columbia, the final barrier to the broad, swift, and flat lower Columbia. The three-or four-mile trip through this series of chutes and low falls was a repeat of previous days; some hair-raising runs down the rapids and occasional portages around the worst ones while lining the canoes through. One of the men shot a goose just above the Cascades and as it began floating into a chute, an Indian ''plunged! into the water & swam to the Goose and brought it on shore, at the head of the great Suck, as this Indian richly earned the goose I suffered him to keep it which he about half picked and Spited it up with the guts in it to roste.''

Clark wasn't particularly impressed with the Indians along this stretch of the river:

''The Indians on those waters do not appear to be sickly, sore eyes are common and maney have lost their eyes, some one and maney both, they have bad teeth, and the greater perpotion of them have worn their teeth down, maney into the gums. They are rather small high cheeks, women small and homely, maney of them have sweled legs, large about the knees owing to the position in which they set on their hams, They are nearly necked only a piece of leather tied about their breech and a small robe which generally comes to a little below their wastes and scercely sufficently large to cover arround them when confined they are all fond of clothes but more so of Beeds perticularly blue & white beeds. They are durty in the extreme both in their cooking and in their houses.

''they have maney imeges cut in wood, generally in the figure of a man. Those people are high with what they have to sell, and say the white people below give them great Prices for what they sell to them. Their noses are all Pierced, and they wear a white shell maney of which are 2 Inches long pushed thro' the nose. all the women have flat heads pressed to almost a point at top.

They press the female childrens heads between 2 bords when young untill they form the skul as they wish it which is generally verry *flat*. This amongst those people is considered as a great mark of buty, and is practised in all the tribes we have passed on this river more or less. Men take more of the drugery off the women than is common with Indians.''

On November 2, they ran the Cascades, the last of the rapids, and covered twenty-nine miles before setting up camp. The river now was an estimated two and a half miles wide and Clark noticed a definite tidal effect on the water level during the night. They were now in the heart of the famed Pacific Flyway, the route taken by migratory waterfowl between the Arctic and tropics twice each year, and they were able to kill several varieties of ducks and geese almost at will in the ponds and sloughs of the broad bottomlands. They could see the three major volcanic peaks, called the Guardians of the Columbia by the Indians; namely, Mt. Hood in Oregon and Mt. St. Helens and Mt. Adams in Washington.

On November 4 they camped near the mouth of the Willamette River but did not realize the river existed until their return trip. They found a large encampment of Indians and counted fifty-two canoes pulled up on the shore. Soon after they set up camp, ''Several canoes of Indians from the village above came down, dressed for the purpose as I supposed of Paying us a friendly visit, they had scarlet & blue blankets Salor Jackets, overalls, Shirts and hats independent of their usial dress! . . . Those fellows we found assumeing and disagreeable, however we Smoked with them and treated them with every attention & friendship.

''dureing the time we were at dinner those fellows Stold my pipe Tomahawk which they were Smoking with, I imediately serched every man and the canoes, but could find nothing of my Tomahawk, while Serching for the Tomahawk one of those Scoundals Stole a cappoe (coat) of one of our interperters, which was found Stufed under the root of a tree, near the place they Sat, we became much displeased with those fellows, which they discovered and moved off on their return home to their village.''

The remainder of the trip down the Columbia was relatively uneventful. They were now in the coastal zone with its frequent and steady rain punctuated by overcast days and damp winds. Even though the temperature here seldom drops below freezing, the constant dampness with no sun to dry clothing can make life miserable, and Clark's journal repeatedly stated a variation of the theme, "we are all wet cold and disagreeable, rain continues & increases." That was to be their sad song they sang until the following spring.

On November 7 they thought they were finally at the ocean and Clark wrote, "Great joy in camp   we are in *view* of the *Ocian, (in the morning when fog cleared off just below last village (first on leaving this village) of Warkiacum)* this great Pacific Octean which we have been so long anxious to See, and the roreing or noise made by the waves brakeing on the rockey Shores (as I suppose) may be heard distinctly."

Alas, they still were not on the ocean. The Columbia River has an average width of four miles, even eight or more in places, and a strong wind will kick up waves similar to that of the ocean. They still had about twenty miles to go before they were on saltwater. In the meantime they had their share of problems from the weather. The tide sometimes battered their canoes against the rocks, and they were fearful of losing everything perishable from the rain. Canoes sometimes sank while tied to the shore, and they had to move camp back into the woods when the tide came in behind a strong wind that threw the logs around on which they were camped.

When they finally reached a campsite at Point Ellice, opposite Astoria, Oregon, they were at the Pacific and they were to stay in the area ten days, until November 25. Colter had found a sandy beach about four miles downriver and around a sharp bend near Chinook Point, with a Chinook Indian camp of thirty-six board houses nearby.

"It would be distressing to See our Situation," Clark wrote plaintively at one point, "all wet and colde our bedding also wet. . . . The rainey weather continued without a longer intermition than 2 hours at a time, from the 5th in the morng untill the 16th is *eleven* days of rain, and the most disagreeable time I have experenced confined on a tempiest coast wet, where I can neither git out to hunt, return to a better situation, or proceed on. . . . I arose early this morning from under a Wet blanket caused by a Shower or rain which fell in the latter part of the last night."

And so it went. Clark continued his duties as surveyor and mapmaker and drew quite accurate maps of the Columbia estuary. The Chinook Indians accompanied them on all their day trips. Clark then began writing accounts of the Chinooks' abilities as traders and bargained for a gift: "one of the Indians had on a roab made of 2 Sea Otter Skins   the fur of them were more butiful than any fur I had ever Seen   both Capt. Lewis & myself endeavored to purchase the *roab* with different artic- les   at length we precured it for a belt of blue beeds which the Squar-wife of our Interpreter Shabono wore around her waste." Nothing was said about Sacajawea's feelings on the matter, but the Indians there were particularly fond of blue beads and the supply was almost gone.

On Thursday, November 21, Clark made one of his more humorous and poignant entries while describing the local Chinook Indians:

"An old woman & Wife to a Cheif of the Chunnooks came and made a Camp near ours. She brought with her 6 young Squars (*her daughters & nieces*) I believe for the purpose of Gratifying the passions of the men of our party and receiving for those indulgences Such Small (presents) as She (the old woman) thought proper to accept of.

"Those people appear to View Sensuality as a Necessary evel, and do not appear to abhor it as a Crime in the unmarried State. The young females are found of the attention of our men and appear to meet the sincere approbation of their friends and connections, for thus obtaining their favours, the Womin of the Chinnook Nation have handsome faces low and badly made with large legs & thighs which are generally Swelled from a Stopage of the circulation in the feet (which are Small) by maney Strands of Beeds or curious Strings which are drawn tight around the leg above the ankle, their legs are also picked (tat- tooed) with defferent figures, I saw on the left arm of a Squar the following letters F. Bowman . . . maney of the Chinnooks ap- pear to have Venerious and pustelus disorders. one woman whome I saw at the Creek appeared all over in Scabs and ulsers &c. . . .

"we divided some ribin between the men of our party to bestow on their favourite Lasses, this plan to save the knives & more valueable articles." One wonders who had been "losing" the silverware.

Their first order of business was setting up a winter camp and building a fortress so they could keep track of their belongings among the less than noble Indians and have dry places to sleep. The requirements for such a camp included a place where there was adequate game for food and good timber available for the building and fires. From the Chinooks they learned that the south side of the river might be a better place to establish a camp. The north shore of the Columbia estuary is sandier and heavy timber is several miles from the coast.

Unlike other decisions, Lewis and Clark put this matter to a vote in the most democratic tradition, and the men voted in favor of going across the river to explore that area. Shields cast the lone dissenting vote; he wanted to head back upriver and spend the winter at the mouth of the Sandy River in the Oregon Cascades' foothills. All the others wanted to get away from the windswept north shore, and Janey, Clark's nickname for Sacajawea, wanted to go anywhere there were "potas", or camas roots.

On November 26, they paddled across the river and camped near Tongue Point but found it a poor place to set up quarters, and the next day they went around Tongue Point and down the south, or Oregon, side of the river. They met some Indians, eleven of them in three canoes, who wanted exorbitant prices for mats and skins. The explorers weren't buying, but the Indians were stealing — an ax to be specific. "I smamed [shamed] this fellow verry much and told them they should not proceed with us,"

The next day was absolutely miserable: "This is our present situation! truly disagreeable. aded to this the robes of our selves and men are all rotten from being continually wet, and we cannot precure others, or blankets in these places. about 12 oClock the wind shifted about to the N.W. and blew with great violence for the remainder of the day   at that I expected every moment to see trees taken up by the roots, some were blown down. Those squals were suckceeded by rain   O! how Tremendious is the day. This dreadful wind and rain continued with intervales of fair weather, the greater part of the evening and night."

On November 29, Lewis took the Indian canoe, which could slice through the waves easier than the others, and loaded it with five of the best men — Drouillard (of course), John Colter, Reuben Field, young Shannon (who by now had been lost three times but showed pluck), and Labiche — and set out in search of a decent place to camp. Clark stayed in camp with the rest of the men, and he didn't enjoy it in the least. He was at one of his lowest moments: "The winds are from Such points that we cannot form our Camp So as to prevent the Smoke which is emencely disagreeable, and painful to the eyes.'' Then, as if catching himself, he added that ''The Shore below the point at our camp is formed of butifull pebble of various colours.''

With Lewis gone, the men had little to do but sit and wait in the rain. The next day several of them, including Clark, were complaining of ''a looseness and griping which I contribute to the diet, pounded fish mixed with Salt water, I derect that in the future that the party mix the pounded fish with fresh water. The squar gave me a piece of bread made of flour which She had reserved for her child and carefully Kept untill this time, which has unfortunately got wet, and a little Sour. this bread I eate with great satisfaction, it being the only mouthfull I had tasted for Several months past.''

Sitka mountain ash *(Pyrus sambucifolia)*

He kept busy, though, and found several different species of wild rose, some ash, alder, the madrona (*Arbutus menziesii*), and took samples of each to send to Washington.

When Lewis had not returned by December 5, Clark expressed deep concern for his safety and wrote that ''a 1000 conjectures had crouded into my mind respecting his probably

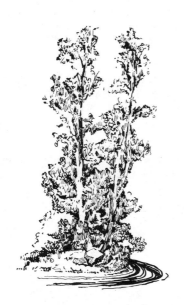

Red alder *(Alnus rubra)*

Roosevelt's elk *(Cervus canadensis roosevelti)*

Madrone *(Arbutus menziessi)*

situation & safty.'' But he returned that day with the men ''haveing found a good situation and Elk sufficent to winter on, his party killed 6 Elk & 5 Deer in their absence. . . .'' The site was downriver beyond the hill and harbor of present-day Astoria, Oregon and about three miles up the Lewis and Clark River. There, in a thick growth of spruce and fir which offered protection from the wind and ample building material, they established their winter quarters.

6

Winter at Fort Clatsop

The day after their arrival, December 8, Clark took off with five men both to search for a good route to the ocean and to blaze a road back so they could set up a salt-making operation. They first followed a ridge as far as they could, then dropped down into marshes and came to a stream which they had to cross in a makeshift raft. They were able to kill an elk, eat it, and then use the skin for a shelter that night, which did not keep out much rain. They met some friendly Clatsop Indians, who "appeared much Neeter in their diat than Indians are Comonly, and frequently wash theer faces and hands.'' He gave them a distinct thrill when he shot a brant, or Canada goose, on the wing. They shared a camp with them that night, but ''I had not been long on my mats before I was attacked most Violently by the flees and they kept up a close Siege dureing the night.''

After concluding that the camp was about seven miles from the ocean, and failing to find a place suitable for a salt cairn, Clark took his men back to the building site where the rest of the party was busy felling trees and clearing land for their winter home.

The fort was completed on December 30 and they named it Fort Clatsop in honor of the Indians around them. It was about fifty feet square with two facing longhouse-style cabins divided into compartments. The roofs of both slanted toward the center parade ground, with the high point at rear forming part of the palisade. Each end was blocked off by posts sunk into the ground, with a large gate at one end and a smaller ''water gate'' at the other. The latter provided a shortcut to a spring that ran about thirty yards from the fort. One side of the fort was divided into three separate rooms for the enlisted men. The other had

Fort Clatsop

four rooms: one for the captains, one for the Charbonneau family of three, an orderly room, and a meathouse.

Clark's entry for Christmas Day, 1805, is one of the most famous of the trip, and one which the tourism boosters of the Columbia estuary have despaired over for decades:

"at day light this morning we were awoke by the discharge of the fire arms of all our party & a Selute, Shouts and a Song which the whole party joined in under our windows, after which they retired to their rooms were chearfull all the morning. after brackfast we divided our Tobacco which amounted to 12 carrots one half of which we gave to the men of the party who used tobacco, and to those who doe not use it we make a present of a handerchief. The Indians leave us in the evening all the party Snugly fixed in their huts. I recved a present of Capt. L. of a fleece hosrie (hosiery) Shirt Draws and Socks, a pr. Mockersons of Whitehouse a Small Indian basket of Gutherich, two Dozen white weazils tails of the Indian woman, & some black root of the Indians before their departure. Drewyer informs me that He saw a Snake pass across the parth today. The day proved Showery wet and disagreeable.

"we would have Spent this day the nativity of Christ in feasting, had we any thing either to raise our Sperits or even gratify our appetites, our Diner concisted of pore Elk, so much Spoiled that we eate it thro' mear necessity, Some Spoiled pounded fish and a fiew roots."

Sergeant Gass pointed out in his journal that they didn't even have salt with which to season the "pore" meat.

On December 28 they sent Joseph Field, Bratton, and Gibson off to make salt with instructions to go southwest, rather than due west as Clark had attempted, because they thought it would be an easier route. They were able to follow some low ground and stream courses until they arrived at the site of present-day Seaside, Oregon and built a salt cairn a short distance from Tillamook Head. The cairn site is one of the few Lewis and Clark sites remaining, and it is located a short distance from the long, sandy beach in a grove of trees. The men were gone several days, long enough for the rest of the expedition to worry about them; two finally returned on January 5 with the craved-for salt. From then on the men rotated the salt-making assignment and reported no problem with the Killamuck [Tillamook] Indians living nearby. It was a pleasant chore. They simply stoked fires under kettles filled with saltwater until the water boiled away, leaving the salt.

On January 1, 1806, Lewis's copy of the Orderly Book shows how thorough the commanders were regarding the running of the fort and the conduct of the party. The long order established or reestablished the chain of command and told the men to be friendly but firm with the local Indians. They were not to "abuse, assault or strike them; unless such abuse assault or stroke be first given by the natives." They were to keep Indians out of the fort at night and if one refused to leave, he was to be thrown out and refused entry afterward. After the guards were relieved from their watch, they were to furnish two loads of wood for the commanding officer's fire. Most of the orders, however, dealt with their relationship with the Indians, and in all cases the men were to treat them well but to demand respect in return.

Most of the three-and-a-half months they spent at Fort Clatsop was devoted simply to seeing to their immediate needs, including securing food, working on equipment, trading with the Indians for food and equipment they would need on the return voyage, and — for the leaders — making copious notes on the surrounding flora and fauna and studying the Indians with an anthropologist's eye. The men weren't terribly happy during the winter, and a certain amount of complaining and sulking was inevitable among men of action reduced to skinning, tanning, and sewing leather clothing. They made more than 300 pairs of moccasins that winter and the men considered such activities women's work.

Mountain quail *(Oreortyx pictus pictus)*

Most of the men would gladly have traded the constant rain of the Pacific coast for the frigid climate of Fort Mandan. And they didn't think too highly of the choice of women among either the Clatsops or the other tribes that came calling. Many were obviously diseased and they were lacking in the ladylike manners of the girls back home. By this time Lewis had resumed the business of writing a journal, and on January 6 he made these observations on the local Indians:

"with us their conversation generally turns upon the subjects of trade, smoking, eating or their women; about the latter they speak without reserve in their presents, of their every part, and of the most formiliar connection. they do not hold the virtue of their women in high estimation, and will even prostitute their wives and daughters for a fishinghook or a stran of beads. . . ."
A few days later Lewis again wrote of their habits, with a touch of humor that perhaps was unintentional.

> The Clatsops Chinnooks and others inhabiting the coast and country of this neighbourhood, are excessively fond of smoking tobacco. in the act of smoking they appear to swallow it as they draw it from the pipe. and for many draughts together you will not perceive the smoke which they take from the pipe; in the same manner also they inhale it in their lungs untill they become surcharged with this vapour when they puff it out to a great distance through their nostrils and mouth; I have no doubt the smoke of the tobacco in this manner becomes much more intoxicating and that they do possess themselves of all it's virtues in their fullest extent; they freequently give us sounding proofs of it's creating a dismorallity of order in the abdomen, nor are those light matters thought indelicate in either sex, but all take the liberty of obeying the dictates of nature without reserve. these people do not appear to know the uce of speprituous liquors, they never having once asked us for it;

> The dress of the women consists of a robe, tissue, and sometimes when the weather is uncommonly cold, a vest. their robe is much smaller than that of the men, never reaching lower than the waist nor extending in front sufficiently for to cover the body. it is like that of the men, confined across the breast with a string and hangs loosly over the sholders and back. the most esteemed and valu-

Sea otter *(Enhydra lutris nereis)*

able of these robes are made of strips of the skins of the
Sea Otter net together with the bark of the white cedar or
silk-grass. these strips are first twisted and laid parallel
with each other a little distance assunder, and then net or
wove together in such manner that the fur appears equally
on both sides, and unites between the strands. it makes a
warm and soft covering. other robes are formed in a similar manner of the skin of the Rackoon, beaver &c. at other
times the skin is dressed in the hair and woarn without any
further preperation . . . when this vest is woarn the breast
of the woman is concealed, but without it which is almost
always the case, they are exposed, and from the habit of
remaining loose and unsuspended grow to great length,
particularly in aged women in many of whom I have seen
the bubby reach as low as the waist. The garment which
occupys the waist, and behind, cannot properly be denom-
inated a petticoat, in the common acceptation of that term;
it is a tissue of white cedar bark, bruised or broken into
small shreds, which are interwoven in the middle by
means of several cords of the same materials, which serve
as well for a girdle as to hold in place the shreds of bark
which form the tissue, and which shreds confined in the

middle hang with their ends pendulous from the waist, the whole being of sufficient thickness when the female stands erect to conceal those parts usually covered from formiliar view, but when she stoops or places herself in many other attitudes, this battery of Venus is not altogether impervious to the inquisitive and penetrating eye of the amorite.

On January 3, 1806, a group of Indians came to the fort with some roots, berries, three dogs, and a small quantity of fresh blubber to sell to the white men. Lewis said the Indians were especially fond of the whale blubber and that they had bought it from their neighbors to the south, the "Callamucks" after a whale had washed to shore and died. Lewis didn't seem particularly interested, however, and said he preferred dog meat: "our party from necessary having been obliged to subsist some length of time on dogs have now become extreemly fond of their flesh; it is worthy of remark that while we lived principally on the flesh of this anamal we were much more healthy strong and more fleshy than we had been since we left the Buffaloe country. for my own part I have become so perfectly reconciled to the dog that I think it an agreeable food and would prefer it vastly to lean Venison or Elk." But he gave Chief Comowool "a pare of sattin breechies with which he appeared much pleased," in exchange for the blubber.

But the blubber incident wasn't closed. Two days later Alexander Willard and Peter Wiser returned from the salt cairn and said that the Tillamooks had given them a considerable amount of blubber, "part of this blubber they brought with them," Lewis wrote, "it was white & not unlike the fat of Poork, tho' the texture was more spongey and somewhat coarser."

Food was much on Lewis's mind, however, and he expressed deep satisfaction at having salt again for his meat, having gone without it for nearly three weeks. Clark didn't care whether or not he had it, Lewis said, but "for myself I must confess I felt a considerable inconvenience from the want of it; the want of bread I consider as trivial provided, I get fat meat, for as to the species of meat I am not very particular, the flesh of the dog the horse and the wolf, having from habit become equally formiliar with any other, and I have learned to think that if the chord by sufficiently strong, which binds the soul and boddy together, it dose not so much matter about the materials which compose it."

Their appetites were whetted by a change of menu and the same day that Willard and Wiser brought the blubber to the fort, Clark decided to organize a trip to trade for more. He prepared a pile of barter goods and selected twelve men and two canoes to make the trip.

They set out the next morning with two more passengers. Both Charbonneau and Sacajawea wanted to go, and it was Sacajawea's eloquent argument that won them a place in the roster. Lewis wrote that "the Indian woman was very importunate to be permitted to go, and was therefore indulged! she observed that she had traveled a long way with us to see the great waters, and that now that monstrous fish was also to be seen, she thought it very hard she could not be permitted to see either (she had never yet been to the Ocean)."

Clark and the party set out up the river and Clark was certain the series of small streams flowing through the area joined the Necanicum River, which flows near the site of the salt cairn. When they entered the bay in search of an Indian guide to take them south, they met strong winds and had to pull over and sit it out. He gave up on hiring an Indian guide and entered a maze of marshes and creeks and followed one of them south as far as he could, then completed the thirty-odd mile overland route on foot. Later-generation students of the exploration, attempting to follow the route in boats, have found frequent portaging and canoe dragging to be necessary.

They arrived at the salt cairn the next day and Clark found a young Indian to guide them over Tillamook Head with the down payment of a file and a promise of other payment on return. They followed the coastline around the curving beach until they reached rocky areas at the foot of the thickly timbered mountain. "my guide made a Sudin halt, pointed to the top of the mountain and uttered the word *Pe shack* which means bad, and made signs that we could not proceed any further on the rocks, but must pass over that mountain, I hesitated a moment & view this emence mountain the top of which was obscured in the clouds, and the assent appeard to be almost perpindecular; as the small Indian parth allong which they had brought emence loads but a fiew hours before, led up this mountain and appeared to assend in a Sideling direction, I thought more than probably that the assent might be torerably easy and therefore proceeded on."

After scrambling up the steep trail, undoubtedly wet from the

Double-crested cormorant *(Phalacrocorax auritus auritus)*

almost constant rain and fog that strikes high headlands along the coast, they met fourteen Indian men and women loaded with blubber from the whale. They camped that night on the mountain, and the next morning Clark stood on its edge and saw the coastline both north and south from where he stood and the seemingly endless Pacific Ocean stretched out at his feet. But when they descended the mountain and walked along the beach to the Indian camp at what is today Cannon Beach, they found only the skeleton left, ''the Whale was already pillaged of every Valuable part'' and the Indians busily boiling the blubber in a large wooden trough with hot stones. When the oil was extracted, they poured it in bladders made from the whale's intestines. Clark was able to purchase only about 300 pounds of

127

Bigleaf maple *(Acer macrophyllum)*

blubber and a few gallons of oil. "Small as this stock is I prise it highly; and thank providence for directing the whale to us; and think him much more kind to us than he was to jonah, having Sent this Monster to be *Swallowed by us* in Sted of *Swallowing of us* as jonah's did."

There was a large commotion in camp that night. While Clark was smoking with the Indians, they heard a "loud Srill voice from the cabins on the opposite side" of the small creek that enters the ocean there, and a quick head count showed that McNeal was missing. An Indian from another village had invited McNeal into his lodge to get something to eat. Inside, a woman gave him some blubber, and then the Indian invited McNeal into another lodge to get "something better," apparently a euphemism for a woman. The woman in the lodge was a friend of McNeal's from the Fort Clatsop area and since she knew what the Indian man had in mind, she and another woman began screaming for help. The Indian fled and Clark credited the women with preventing the "horred act."

On January 9, Clark's party began the return trip with the oil and blubber divided among the members of the party, and on the way they passed a group of Indians also loaded with oil and blubber. One of the women slipped on a steep slope and her load came off her back. Clark went to help and was amazed to find that her load was "as much as I could lift and must exceed 100 lbs." They spent that night with the salt party and swapped stories about their experiences with the local Indians.

The following morning they left early and arrived back at Fort Clatsop at 10 o'clock that night.

The journey to Cannon Beach was to be the highlight of the winter. The rest of the time was spent working on the journals

Whistling swans *(Olor columbianus)*

and worrying about food. Their journals for this period are much more complete and detailed than those from the winter at Fort Mandan, mainly because they had much more to work with. There really wasn't much new to report from the upriver trip to Mandan because most of the basic knowledge about the land and the people was already somewhere in print. But the trip from Mandan to Fort Clatsop was virgin territory for all the sciences, and the captains' writings on the flora and fauna and the Indians that winter were as important to science as were those findings of Captain Cook on his journeys. The Mandan material runs only about seventy pages in the journals; the Fort Clatsop writings cover more than 320 pages.

Clark worked frequently on his maps of the area they covered, and both leaders decorated their journals with drawings that range from the precise pictures of various fish to tools and implements used by the local tribes. They drew pictures of digging tools made of elk horn fabricated by the local tribe, their cedar hats, their fish knives, their various canoe designs and how they were constructed; they also drew pictures of the various plant and bird life. The two captains thus reflected the breadth and depth of the interests of the man who chose and trained them for the expedition, Thomas Jefferson. It is impossible to think that Jefferson could have been disappointed in their reports, just as it is impossible to think of two men of such varied talents being found today to lead such an expedition.

Consider for a moment their talents. They were expert hunters and rivermen. They were superb leaders. They were trained in all the necessary sciences — medicine, zoology, anthropology, botany, astronomy, navigation. They were diplomats of the highest order and in spite of Clark's wild spelling, both men were excellent writers. They were artists. And perhaps most important of all, they were highly resourceful. No situations arose that they could not survive. They had that devotion to duty that transcends merely following orders. They simply believed in doing their job as well as they could, no matter how trying the circumstances. One wonders, after reading the journals and other material of the two men, if they ever realized how brilliant they really were. It is doubtful they ever thought of themselves as anything other than fortunate to have the opportunity to make the trip.

There can be no parallel to their expedition until men are sent into outer space with no more guidance after leaving the earth than their own resourcefulness and courage.

But such matters certainly were not on their minds while they were waiting for winter to end and the return trip to begin. They were more concerned with the immediate chores, and they can be forgiven for complaining so much about the bad food, constant cold rain, and illness that seemed to plague them all winter. Nearly every man in the company was ill at one time or another during that dreary winter, and there were many days when the hunters returned without an elk, even though there were vast herds of them in that corner of Oregon.

7

Fort Clatsop to Travelers Rest

At last, on Saturday, March 22, 1806, they were ready to head back over the route they had followed to the Pacific the previous year. They spent that final day making all the preparations, and of course rain fell all day and kept them from making some necessary repairs on canoes. Rather than wait another day, they decided to leave and fix the leaks enroute. Chief Comowool came by on that last day and Lewis and Clark gave him their houses and furniture because, as Lewis wrote, "he has been much more kind and hospitable to us than any other indian in this neighbourhood."

On Sunday, March 23, "the rain seased and it became fair about Meridian, at which time we loaded our canoes & at 1 P.M. left Fort Clatsop on our homeward bound journey." They soon were met by a group of men and an "old boud" with six prostitutes. The Indians had a canoe, a sea otter pelt, and some hats for sale in addition to the girls. The company bought only the sea otter pelt.

The next day they took a wrong turn in the vast delta and were headed up a dead-end slough when a Calamet Indian saw them and guided them back into the main channel. Then, to their chagrin, he pointed to a canoe they were using and said it belonged to him. They believed him because back at Fort Clatsop after Clatsop Indians had stolen some of their precious if "pore" elk meat, they had retaliated by taking an Indian canoe. But the owner wasn't upset. He was happy to take an elk skin for it, mainly because he had another canoe anyway.

The river bottom of the lower Columbia — the stretch from

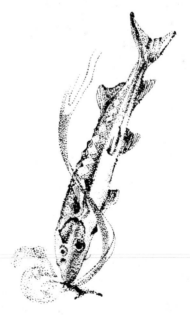

White sturgeon *(Acipenser transmontanus)*

Salmon (genus *Oncorhynchus*)

the Cascades to the sea that is subject to the tides — is often flat and offered the party few dry places to camp. They found sufficient game to kill and were able to buy arrowhead roots (wappato), eulachon (smelt), and occasionally sturgeon from the Indians who lined the banks. But food was a matter of concern to them, and at one time they even considered waiting on the lower river for a month until the salmon started running so as to be certain they should have enough to last them through the Bitterroots. This idea was discarded almost as soon as it was put forth, however. They did not relish the thought of being trapped by ice somewhere on the upper Missouri; the river Indians were insolent and insulting and pilfered everything they could lay hands on — tools, knives, tomahawks. They even tried to steal Lewis' big Newfoundland dog, Scannon!

By the time they found and passed the Willamette River and stopped upriver at the Washougal, they were feeling better about the food situation. They were far enough ahead on their killing to jerk the meat of several bear, some elk, and deer and now felt secure since they could always trade for additional horses to take along for their meat.

It took them ten arduous days to portage around the Cascades, the Narrows, and finally Celilo Falls. They had constant trouble with the Indians along this stretch of river and for decades — if not a century later — other white men were to make similar observations about the tribes that controlled this turbid stretch of the river. The Indians were very jealous of their fishing rights in this area, and they built those marvelous, rickety platforms directly over the falls that always looked like tragedies in process. Up until the day the backwaters of Bonneville Dam covered this spectacular portion of the Columbia, the Indians were still jealously guarding their birthright.

Indian netting salmon at Celilo Falls, Columbia River

Grand fir *(Abies grandis)*

When they reentered the horse country above Hood River —
Indians below in the coastal zone had no use for horses because
they relied entirely on water for transporation, and fodder was
scarce in the thick timber — the explorers were faced with a
problem: they had virtually no trade goods left. Finally, however, they were able to trade three kettles for five horses.

Then Clark, ever resourceful, found a solution. He had
treated the wife of a chief, "a sulky Bitch" with back pains.
When the camphor and flannel seemed to give her relief, Clark
"accepted" two horses as payment. From then on, Dr. William
Clark held office hours wherever they went, and their livestock
multiplied. But when the haggling was over at Hood River, they
still had only ten horses while they considered a dozen to be the
minimum. Consequently they were forced to go partly by water
and partly by land. They used nine of the horses as pack animals
and put the ailing Bratton on the tenth. Then they put Colter,
Potts, Gass, and Reuben Field in charge of two canoes and
resumed the march eastward.

135

Mountain hemlock *(Tsuga mertensiana)*

On April 21 they were joined by a lone Nez Percé they knew from the previous year, and two days later a Nez Percé family joined them. They decided it was impossible to follow the river past the remainder of the rapids, so they broke up some canoes for firewood and sold the others to local Indians. Then they took to the horses, climbed out of the gorge onto the high ground, and headed toward the Clearwater.

Six days later they met the chief, Yellept, and his Walla Wallas, with whom they had struck up a warm friendship on the way downriver, and they decided to stay with them three days. He provided them, without the usual cost, with firewood and food and sold them a pack of dogs. During the three-day rest and festival a group of Yakimas numbering about 100 came down, and each night the whole gathering danced to the music of Cruzatte's fiddle.

The interpretation was of the usual round-robin sort with a Shoshoni woman prisoner translating from Walla Walla to Shoshoni to Sacajawea, who put it into Minitari for Charbon-neau, who finally turned it into English, then vice versa. It is little wonder that the long, convoluted, and even poetic speeches of the Indians that were written down fifty years later do not appear in the explorers' journals. By the time the statements were filtered through three or four languages, only the essence remained.

Once they got under way again, they had to swim their horses from the northern, or Washington, side of the Columbia across to the mouth of the Walla Walla River and used two canoes loaned by Yellept to transfer their baggage and the nonswimmers. Then, with their herd of horses now numbering twenty-three, they set out overland on a shortcut of which the Indians had told them. The trail, or road as they called it, swung south of the Snake River canyon, much to their delight, and headed almost due east across the rolling, barren plains of southwest Washington. The trail took them through the present-day towns of Dayton and Waitsburg, and there were sufficient small streams, including the Touchet River, to provide them with water.

Once they were back in Nez Percé country, they felt more at ease among the Indians. But there were some Indians who did not impress easily, and there was an incident on May 5 that could have ruined their rapport with them. Lewis tells the story succinctly:

"while at dinner an indian fellow verry impertinently threw a poor half starved puppy nearly in my plait by way of derision for our eating dogs and laughed very heartily at his own impertinence; I was so provoked at his insolence that I caught the puppy and threw it with great violence at him and struck him in the breast and face, siezed my tomahawk and shewed him by signs if he repeated his insolence I would tommahawk him, the fellow withdrew apparently much mortifyed and I continued my repast *on dog* without further molestation."

They reached Canoe Camp on the Clearwater River May 7, and an Indian was waiting for them with two canisters of powder that a dog had dug up from the cache the past fall shortly after they left. They naturally were pleased and surprised that the man had gone to so much trouble to keep it for them.

Then they discovered that they had hurried eastward for no good reason; the snow was still too deep in the Bitterroots for them to cross Lolo Pass. They had no choice but to establish a permanent camp while waiting. They didn't give a name to their camp, but it has since taken on one of two names, either Camp Long or Camp Chopunnish, the latter which the party called the Nez Percé.

As usual, food was a major problem and the men's stomachs would not accept roots as a steady diet, even though the men were told that toward the end of the past winter the Indians had resorted to boiling moss and lichen off trees. One of the chiefs,

Broken Arm, who had been absent the previous fall, off fighting a war somewhere, told them to kill any of the horses running loose at no charge.

The month they stayed there was occupied in the endless search for food, running games with the Indians, and Dr. Clark's "medicine show." Even though he could not promise sure cures for all ills, the Indians seemed pleased that he had tried to help them and he ran a regular sick call virtually the entire month they were there. The captains also were able to compile a voluminous report on the tribes in the area, and they were most likely the first white men to see that outstanding breed of spotted horses developed by the Nez Percé, the Appaloosa. So plentiful were horses among the tribe that they made several outright gifts of horses to Lewis and Clark, including the gray and white animals they prized more highly even than the Appaloosa.

By June 13 they could wait around the low country no longer. They sent Reuben Field and Willard ahead to hunt and wait for them with game and prepared to leave. The next day, while making final preparations and hobbling the horses so they wouldn't have to waste most of the day chasing them down, Clark wrote of his forebodings of the trip ahead: "even now I shudder with the expectation with great difficuelties in passing those Mountains, from the debth of snow and the want of grass sufficient to subsist our horses, as about 4 days we Shall be on the top of the Mountain which we have every reason to beleive is covered with snow the greater part of the year."

He was definitely right in his fears. The party left on June 15, with snow drifts twelve to fifteen feet deep, and then gave up the attempt, an action that seemed to plunge Lewis into one of his darker moods:

"here was winter with all it's rigors; the air was cold, my hands and feet benumbed. we knew that it would require five days to reach the fish wears [weirs] at the entrance of Colt Creek, provided we were so fortunate as to be enabled to follow the proper ridges of the mountains to lead us to that place; of this Drewyer our principal dependance as a woodman and guide was entirely doubtful!" Thus defeated for the only time during the trip, in part because they had attempted the crossing without the services of an Indian guide, they gave it up. They cached as much material as they could by hanging it in trees or suspending it on poles between trees and then returned to the valley, "melancholy and disappointed," as Gass wrote later.

But rather than going all the way back, they sent Drouillard and Shannon to the Indians with instructions to hire guides with a rifle as payment, and began their own slow descent to a meadow below the snowline. Enroute Colter's horse fell into Hungry Creek and they both were swept down the swift and rocky stream, tumbling over and over together. But the tough woodsman survived without injury and didn't even lose his gun.

Two days later, Drouillard and Shannon returned with three young Indians who agreed to lead them for the price of two additional guns. They set out again on June 24. The trip was as rough as the previous westward journey had been, but often the horses were able to walk on top of the frozen-crusted snow. Six days later, after averaging twenty-six miles a day, they arrived at Travelers Rest. They had stopped earlier that day at Lolo Hot Springs, now a resort, and the men frolicked in the hot mud and water, with Clark being able to stand only ten minutes of the steaming water. They were amazed at the Indians' game of emerging from the hot pools, plunging immediately into the nearly freezing water of a nearby creek, and then diving back in the pools.

The men and pack animals had earned a break, and they spent two days at Travelers Rest making final plans for the next adventure, in one of which Lewis first almost lost his scalp, and then was mistaken for an elk.

8

Lewis Among the Blackfeet

During the winter at Fort Clatsop the leaders had concocted a plan to extend their exploration by splitting the party into three groups: Lewis would follow the shortcut back to the Missouri River and then swing up the Marias to explore it to see if it opened up the Canadian country, as they thought.

A second party led by Sgt. Pryor would take a few men and travel ahead by horseback straight across Montana to Fort Mandan, where he was to authorize the North-West Fur Company's factor, Hugh Heney, to persuade some key chiefs to accompany the expedition to Washington. In return, Heney would be offered a bonus and the promise of consideration for the job of Indian agent among the Sioux.

A third party, led by Clark, would go south from Travelers Rest to Camp Fortunate and recover their cached goods, including the boats, and strike out overland to intercept the upper Yellowstone. At Three Forks Clark would send still another party to meet Lewis at Great Falls. They all would meet again at the mouth of the Yellowstone, except Pryor, who would already be in the Mandan villages.

We can dispose of the Pryor expedition quickly because it was a failure. Pryor accompanied Clark to Camp Fortunate, then struck out with three men overland. They were out only two days before their mission ended. A party of Crow Indians stole their horses and they were reduced to boatmen again. They walked nearly halfway across Montana to Pompeys Pillar, where they were able to kill some buffalo. They stretched the hides over a wooden framework to build a bullboat, then started paddling down the Yellowstone, four men in a tub with the second tub behind as a reserve. They caught up with Clark's group on August 8, cheerful and none the worse from the long march.

Lewis' trip was another matter.

On July 1, 1806, Lewis called for volunteers to accompany him on a trip they all knew was potentially the most hazardous of the three. Of the men who stepped forward Lewis selected only six: Drouillard, both Field brothers, Werner, Frazier, and Gass. The next day his trip almost came to an end when a horse

Buffalo herd

A Mandan bullboat made of buffalo hide and willow frame

fell under him and they tumbled forty feet down a mountainside, but he rose unhurt.

The small party left on July 3, with three additional men to accompany them only as far as the Great Falls — Thompson, McNeal, and Goodrich — who were to stay there to dig up the cache, make the portage, and put the gear in order. They also took along five Nez Percé guides and seventeen horses and camped the first night near what is today Missoula, Montana. The guides were to go no farther than the Hellgate area because of hostile tribes ahead, which Lewis appreciated, and after smoking a farewell pipe with them, the white men were on their own among the Blackfeet.

They went overland to the Sun River, then descended it to the Missouri near the cached goods above the falls. They built boats of buffalo skin and crossed the Missouri, leaving Drouillard behind to chase some Blackfeet who had stolen seven horses. He returned empty-handed but with information on the location of camps.

Just before dark that night, July 15, McNeal returned to camp with a harrowing story and a musket broken at the breach. He had ridden within ten feet of a grizzly without seeing him. The frightened horse turned and threw McNeal at the feet of the bear. The bear was apparently startled and didn't swat McNeal fast enough. McNeal rose and "with his clubbed musquet he struck the bear over the head and cut him with the guard of the gun and broke off the breech, the bear stunned with the stroke fell to the ground and began to scratch his head with his feet; this gave McNeal time to climb a willow tree which was near at hand and thus fortunately made his escape. the bear waited at the foot of the tree untill late in the evening before he left him . . . these bear are a most tremenduous animal; it seems that the hand of providence has been most wonderfully in our favor with rispect to them, or some of us would long since have fallen a sacrifice to their farosity. there seems to be a sertain fatality attatched to the neighbourhood of these falls, for there is always a chapter of accedents prepared for us during our residence at them."

The next day they saddled up and rode down to the falls after swimming the river above White Bear Island, which they had named the previous year because grizzlies seemed to like the island. Lewis made a hurried sketch of one of the falls and noted that the water level was lower than it had been the previous June.

On July 17, they struck out across the open country along the Marias River and passed the trail of a wounded and bleeding buffalo, set up camp that night in a thickly wooded area beside the Teton River, a Marias tributary, and sent Drouillard back to track the wounded buffalo. Lewis was expecting the worst from the Blackfeet and wrote that "as they are a vicious lawless and reather an abandoned set of wretches I wish to avoid an interview with them if possible. I have no doubt but they would steel our horses if they have it in their power and finding us weak should they happen to be numerous wil most probably attempt to rob us of our arms and baggage." They each took turns standing guard at night, including, for a change, Lewis himself.

On Monday, July 21, they reached a fork in the Marias and Lewis chose the northern stream, Cut Bank Creek. They were unable to find timber for fire at camp that night, and built one of buffalo chips. The next day they went farther up the stream and Lewis finally gave up his opinion that they were on a route to the Saskatchewan River. He thought it unnecessary to proceed farther and decided to camp in a clump of cottonwood and take a couple of days both to rest the horses and to replenish their larder. They had wounded buffalo the two previous days but were unable to catch them because their horses were so tired.

The next day Drouillard, while out hunting, found an abandoned Indian camp of eleven lodges, but the hunters were unable to bring back any food. It was virtually the same the next day, July 24, except that they killed some pigeons. Fortunately there was abundant grass at the camp for the horses.

On July 25 Lewis had had enough of the area and was ready to leave for the Missouri again. He had stayed a day longer than planned because he had been unable to establish the longitude of the camp due to cloudy weather. Lewis was reluctant to stay any longer because he wanted to reach St. Louis that fall.

Buffalo

Then on the weekend of July 26–27 Lewis and his small group almost ended their trip in those rolling, barren, and rather bleak plains of northern Montana.

They departed their camp, aptly named Camp Disappointment, and after going a few miles split up, with Drouillard riding off to one side of them several hundred yards. Then Drouillard headed down to the Marias River with Lewis and the Fields' brothers keeping to the high ground. When they topped a high ridge, Lewis spotted several horses and Indians atop another hill, looking down at Drouillard. Lewis noted that several horses were saddled and he feared that Drouillard would be attacked. He had Joseph Field unfurl the flag and they approached the Indians slowly.

The Indians rounded up their mounts and Lewis counted about an equal number of Indians as horses. When they were about a quarter of a mile apart, a single Indian "mounted his horse and rode full speed towards us, which when I discovered I halted and alighted from my horse; he came within a hundred paces halted looked at us and turned his horse about and returned as briskly to his party as he had advanced; while he halted near us I held out my hand and becconed to him to approach but he paid no attention to my overtures. on his return to his party they all decended the hill and mounted their horses and advanced toward us leaving their horses behind them, we also advanced to meet them. I counted eight of them but still supposed that there were others concealed as there were several other horses saddled. I told the two men with me that I apprehended that these were the Minnetares of Fort de Prarie and from their known character I expected that we were to have some difficulty with them. . . ."

The meeting started without mishap. They greeted each other normally and when the Indians said they wanted to smoke with them, Lewis said his other man, Drouillard, had his pipe and suggested that since they had probably seen him last, they send a man with one of the Field brothers to him. While they were gone, Lewis asked if there were a chief among them and they said there were three. He didn't believe them but gave to one a medal, to another a flag, and to a third a handkerchief. Then Lewis decided they were more alarmed at the chance meeting than he and his men and concluded there were only the eight Indians rather than the thirty he originally thought he saw.

Then Lewis made a blunder. He suggested that since it was late in the day they move down to the river and camp together. They rode down the steep, loose banks to the Marias and set up a camp where three lone trees stood. The Indians erected a large semicircle of buffalo skins for shelter and invited the men to join them. Lewis and Drouillard did, but the Field brothers stayed outside by the fire. They ate together and smoked until late in the night while Lewis told them of his mission and offered to pay a young Indian ten horses and some tobacco to go with them to the mouth of the Maria for a conference with their chiefs. He took the first watch that night and at 11 P.M. woke Reuben Field and told him to watch the Indians very carefully and to wake the rest of the party if any tried to sneak away in the night.

The next morning the Indians crowded around the fire and Joseph Field, who was on guard, laid his gun down behind him, paying slight attention to the Indians. One sneaked behind him and took his gun and that of Reuben, which was lying nearby. It was a carefully rehearsed scene because at the same time two of the other Indians grabbed Lewis' and Drouillard's guns.

Joseph Field saw the Indians running away with the two guns and called his brother. They gave chase and caught them fifty or sixty yards away and retrieved the guns. Then Reuben stabbed one of the Indians in the heart, and he fell dead after running another fifteen steps. The Field boys immediately ran back to camp to help out there.

Drouillard was awake and had jumped up and grabbed his gun

back before the Indian was able to get away, but the Indian still had his pouch and the fight between the two men woke Lewis as the tough woodsman shouted, "Damn you, let go my gun!"

Lewis grabbed for his gun, which was gone, then drew his pistol and began to chase the Indian who had taken it. He shouted at him to drop it, which he did. When the Indian stopped, both Fields boys arrived and were going to shoot him until Lewis ordered them to desist.

Lewis then told his men to shoot any Indian who tried to drive off their horses, which some were already in the process of doing. Lewis was so close on their heels that the braves had to leave a dozen of their own horses behind.

"at the distance of three hundred paces they entered one of those steep nitches in the bluff with the horses before them   being nearly out of breath I could pursue no further, I called to them as I had done several times before that I would shoot them if they did not give me my horse and raised my gun, one of them jumped behind a rock and spoke to the other who turned arround and stoped at the distance of 30 steps from me and I shot him through the belly, he fell to his knees and on his wright elbow from which position he partly raised himself up and fired at me, and turning himself about crawled in behind a rock which was a few feet from him. he overshot me, being bearheaded I felt the wind of his bullet very distinctly."

Lewis didn't have his shot pouch with him so he didn't follow the Indians any farther. Rather, "I therefore returned leasurely towards camp," and met Drouillard coming to help him.

They gathered up their gear, took four of the best Indian ponies, and Lewis loaded four shields, two bows, quivers of arrows, and a few other articles because the Indians had left everything behind. He also took the flag he had given them but left the medal around the neck of the dead man as something of a calling card, or warning, so the Indians would know who they were.

Then they made one of the greatest rides in American history. By 3 P.M. that afternoon they had covered more than sixty miles. They took a brief rest and then rode another twenty miles before dark. They stopped, killed a buffalo for dinner, and then struck out again across the rough, gullied landscape and rode by moonlight until they reached the Missouri River at about 2 A.M. near present-day Fort Benton. In a single day, over incredibly rough terrain, they had covered more than 100 miles. "My indian horse carried me very well in short much better than my own would have done and leaves me with but little reason to complain of the robbery,'' Lewis wrote with some satisfaction.

The next morning "proved fair, I slept sound but fortunately awoke as day appeared, I awaked the men and directed the horses to be saddled, I was so soar from my ride yesterday that I could scarcely stand, and the men complained of being in a similar situation however I encouraged them by telling them that our own lives as well as those of our friends and fellow travellers depended on our exertions at this moment.'' The men wanted to head directly to the river and try to meet the men at the "grog spring," the sulfur spring, but Lewis said they must go directly to the mouth of the Marias River, the agreed-on rendezvous point, and put as much distance between them and the Blackfeet as possible.

When they had gone about twelve miles, each mile an agony in their present state, they heard rifle fire and galloped down to the Missouri banks where they saw the canoes coming downstream. It was one of those marvelous coincidences. They "striped our horses and gave them their final discharge imbarking without loss of time with our baggage.''

The cache crew had had no difficulties during the past few days they were separated, other than Wiser's cutting his leg badly. When they reached the cache above the falls, they found it had caved in during the winter, and they lost two bearskins and much of their clothing. But the gunpowder, corn flour, pork, and salt were in good condition. While they were there, Gass and Willard arrived overland from Three Forks with the horses, which they brought to help with the portage around the falls.

From July 29 until August 10, little out of the ordinary happened. They drifted down the river leisurely, stopping occasionally to kill game, either for food or for the skins to give to President Jefferson. They had never had conditions so easy or pleasant. Lewis wanted to hurry along to be sure Clark didn't have to wait for them, but the weather was clement, if occasionally wet from thundershowers — nothing, however, compared with their past winter.

Then Lewis managed to be in the wrong place at the wrong time with the wrong hunter. He and Cruzatte left the river to hunt a herd of elk they spotted from the canoes.

We fired on the Elk I killed one and he wounded another, we reloaded our guns and took different routs through the thick willows in pursuit of the Elk; I was in the act of firing on the Elk a second time when a ball struck my left thye about an inch below my hip joint, missing the bone it passed through the left thye and cut the thickness of the bullet across the hinder part of the right thye; the stroke was very severe; I instantly supposed that Cruzatte had shot me in mistake for an Elk as I was dressed in brown leather and he cannot see very well; under this impression I called out to him damn you, you have shot me, and looked towards the place from whence the ball had come, seeing nothing I called Cruzatte several times as loud as I could but received no answer; I was now preswaded that it was an indian that had shot me as the report of the gun did not appear to be more than 40 paces from me and Cruzatte appeared to be out of hearing of me; in this situation not knowing how many indians there might be concealed in the bushes I thought best to make good my retreat to the perogue, calling out as I ran for the first hundred paces as loud as I could to Cruzatte to retreat that there were indians to allarm him in time to make his escape also; I still retained the charge in my gun which I was about to discharge at the moment the ball struck me. when I arrived in sight of the perogue I called the men to their arms to which they flew in an instant, I told them that I was wounded but I hoped not mortally, by an indian I believed and directed them to follow me that I would return & give them battle and releive Cruzatte if possible who I feared had fallen into their hands; the men followed me as they were bid and I returned about a hundred paces when my wounds became so painfull and my thye so stiff that I could scarcely get on; in short I was compelled to halt and ordered the men to proceed and if they found themselves overpowered by numbers to retreat in order keeping up a fire. I now got back to the perogue as well as I could and prepared my self with a pistol my rifle and air-gun being determined as a retreat was impracticable to sell my life as deerly as possible. in this state of anxiety and suspense I remained about 20 minutes when the party returned with Cruzatte and reported that there were no indians nor the appearance of any; Cruzatte seemed much allarmed and declared if he had shot me it was not his intention, that he had shot an Elk in the willows after he left or seperated from me. I asked him whether he did not hear me when I called to him so frequently which he absolutely denied. I do not beleive that the fellow did it intentionally but after finding that he had shot me was anxious to conceal his knowledge of having done so. the ball had lodged in my breeches which I knew to be the ball of the short rifles such as that he had, and there being no person out with me but him and no indians that we could discover I have no doubt in my own mind of his having shot me.

Lewis spent an uncomfortable night with a high fever, and the next day drifted to the Yellowstone. There they found a note beside the river left by Clark and his crew telling him of Pryor's failure to ride overland to the Mandan villages. Now Lewis had another reason to be glum. When they were reunited on August 12, Lewis said that "as wrighting in my present situation is extreemly painful to me I shall desist untill I recover and leave to my friend Capt. C. the continuation of our journal." But he felt compelled to add a note about a wild cherry that was blooming in the area before signing off. The rest of the journals were in Clark's hand.

9

Clark on the Yellowstone

Clark's trek from Travelers Rest to the mouth of the Yellowstone was almost dull compared with Lewis's adventure on the Marias and the Missouri.

On July 3, 1806, he and his twenty men, plus Sacajawea and Little Pomp, collected their horses, by now increased to fifty, and rode south up the Bitterroot Valley and camped the first night near what is today Corvellis, Montana. They dined that night on a deer and some roots amid swarms of mosquitoes. Clark had to give Potts an opium pill because he was "very unwell . . . oweing to rideing a hard trotting horse." The opium gave him fast relief.

They went as far as Ross's Hole and used a shortcut recommended by the Flatheads that would save at least two days. Instead of going back over Lost Trail Pass and all the trouble that would involve, the trail took them over the Continental Divide at Gibbons Pass. Once they were over into the Big Hole River Valley, Sacajawea was on home ground and she could serve as guide. She led them back to Camp Fortunate five days later, on July 8. Clark estimated the length of the trip at 164 miles.

Shannon failed to get lost during this trek, but he did manage to lose a tomahawk the second day out. Clark sent him back for it alone and he straggled in about sunset, tomahawk in hand.

When they arrived at their cache of canoes and other goods, the men started burrowing like badgers. "the most of the Party with me being Chewers of Tobacco become so impatient to be chewing that they scercely gave themselves time to take their saddles off their horses before they were off to the deposit. I found every article safe, except a little damp. I gave to each man who used tobacco about two feet off a part of a role took one third of the ballance myself and put up 2/3 in a box to send down with the most of the articles which had been left at this place, by the canoes to Capt. Lewis. as it was late nothing could be done with the canoes this evening. I examined them and found them all safe except one of the largest which had a large hole in one Side & Split in bow."

They cut up the damaged canoe, apparently hacked at by an Indian, and used it for paddles and firewood.

They spent the next day, July 9, repairing the canoes and loading them for departure the following day. The trip down the river to Three Forks was easy on the swift Jefferson River, and Pryor and his crew accompanied them along the bank on horseback. One man, Howard, had a narrow escape when the canoe he shared with Clark was driven to shore by a sudden wind. A log projecting from the bank almost crushed him, but he escaped without injury.

Pryor rode on ahead of the canoe team and waited for them at the Three Forks, where they arrived July 13. Clark gave the tobacco for Lewis' group to Ordway and sent him with ten men in the canoes down the Missouri to meet the Gass cache contingent at the Great Falls.

From Three Forks, Clark's party headed overland with the forty-nine horses and one colt, camping the first night near present-day Logan, Montana. Clark was struck by the beauty and richness of the area: "The country in the forks between Gallitins & Madisens rivers is a butifull leavel plain covered with low grass. on the lower or N E Side of Gallitins river the country rises gradually to the foot of a mountain which runs nearly parrelal."

It was Sacajawea who recommended Bozeman Pass and Clark gave her the credit she deserved. "The indian woman who has been of great service to me as a pilot through this country recommends a gap in the mountain more south which I shall cross." The pass Clark considered was Bridger Pass.

Five days later, on July 18, two members of the party were injured in horse accidents. First Charbonneau, thrown when his horse stepped in a hole while chasing a buffalo, received some bruises and cuts. Then Gibson fell while trying to mount his horse and hit a fire-blackened snag he said was an inch in diameter. The snag penetrated his thigh and for several days he couldn't ride or walk. A litter of sorts had to be built that rested on the back of the gentlest horse in the string.

The party followed the Yellowstone for several miles in search of good timber to build their canoes and finally found cottonwoods at a site between present-day Laurel and Columbus, Montana. Gibson still suffered and could stay on a horse only for an hour or two before he had to be taken off to be stretched out on the ground.

On July 20 they started building the canoes. First they had to carve handles for the ax heads, then they set to work felling trees to build two canoes "of 28 feet in length and about 16 or 18 inches deep and from 16 to 24 inches wide. . . . The horses being fatigued and their feet very Sore, I shall let them rest a few days. during which time the party intended for to take them by land to the Mandans will dress their skins and make themselves clothes to ware, as they are nearly naked."

During the five days they were at the canoe camp some Indians made off unseen with half of their horses, and the searching parties Clark sent out yielded nothing. He doubled the guard around the remaining twenty-six head to be sure Pryor's crew bound for the Mandans would have something to ride. The closest they came to an Indian was a worn-out moccasin and dead fires.

On the morning of July 24 the party split up, with Pryor, Shannon, Hall, and Windsor riding out across the rolling plains in a more-or-less straight line for the Mandan villages. Clark and his group of eight headed down the Yellowstone River. With him were York, Charbonneau, Sacajawea and Little Pomp, Bratton, Gibson (whose wound hadn't healed sufficiently to accompany Pryor), Labiche, and Shields.

They lashed the two new dugouts together into something of an outrigger or catamaran configuration and began one of the easiest parts of the whole trip. They passed a large rock standing alone on the south side of the river on July 25 and pulled to the bank to investigate it. Clark immediately named it Pompy's Tower for Sacajawea's son (now called Pompeys Pillar) and climbed to the top of the 200-foot protuberance. They found two piles of stone put there by Indians, and Clark noticed at one spot on the east side some figures of animals carved into the wall. He added his name and the date, and his inscription still shows clearly, although it has to be protected by heavy glass.

Since they had plenty of leisure time on the Yellowstone, Clark drafted a long and involved speech to deliver to Indians should they meet any on the river. The speech outlined the governmental plans for dealing with Indians and showed Clark's considerable abilities as a diplomat. Unfortunately the speech was never delivered because they saw no Indians.

Their major complaint on the float trip was mosquitoes, for the netting they brought from St. Louis was by now riddled with holes big enough for horseflies to walk through.

On the morning of August 8, after Clark had sent Shields and Gibson out to hunt, Pryor, Shannon, Hall, and Windsor came drifting down the river in the buffalo-skin bullboats, much to Clark's surprise and distress. They told Clark of the loss of their horses to the Indians and of how Shannon had killed a buffalo which they had used for meat and a bullboat. The only major problem they had had during the trip was a wolf which came into their camp one night, attacked Pryor, bit his hand, and then made a pass at Windsor before Shannon shot him. Fortunately the predator had not been rabid.

Three days later they met the first white men they'd seen other than their own party since just after leaving Fort Mandan the previous year. They were Joseph Dickson and Forrest Hancock, both trappers from Illinois on their way to the Yellowstone country. The party caught up on the latest news from the United States, with most of the information centering around relationships with Indians.

August 12 was a busy and happy day. But it began with still another Shannon loss — his tomahawk again. Clark, as usual, sent him back to the previous night's camp to retrieve it, and Shields went with the youth. Then at noon, "Capt. Lewis hove in Sight with the party which went by way of the Missouri."

With the party all together again, none of them the worse for the experience except for Lewis and his painful wound in the buttocks, the rest of the trip was almost anticlimactic. One can only guess at the conversations between Lewis and Clark but can assume, with some accuracy, that the rest of the men must have had a few chuckles over Cruzatte's accident with the gun. Clark was defensive about it and wrote that "This Crusat is near Sighted and has the use of but one eye, he is an attentive industrious man and one whome we both have placed the greatest confidence in dureing the whole rout."

That same afternoon the two trappers, Dickson and Hancock, gave up their plans to travel up the Yellowstone, turned around, caught up with the explorers, and returned to the Mandan villages with them. The flotilla immediately struck out down the Missouri, leaving behind Pryor's two precious bullboats.

They stayed in the Mandan villages only three days this time. They were anxious to return to St. Louis, then continue to Washington before winter set in. They found that most of their Fort Mandan had been burned in a prairie fire.

Here Charbonneau and Sacajawea took their farewells. He was paid "$500.33 1/3," plus the price of a horse and lodge. Little Pomp, now nineteen-months-old and the apple of Clark's eye would be missed by all the men. Clark offered to take Little Pomp to St. Louis with him to rear and educate. But he wasn't weaned yet, and the offer was delayed a few years. Clark later kept his promise, and Jean Baptiste Charbonneau became one of the better-known mountain men and guides until his death in Oregon at the age of sixty-one.

Colter also left them at the Mandan villages and headed back up the Yellowstone River with the two trappers, after being paid $179.33 for his services. After his harrowing adventures in the mountains, mentioned earlier, Colter retired with his Indian wife to a farm near that of Daniel Boone at La Charette, Missouri, where he died after only three years of retirement, in 1813.

Lewis and Clark spent part of the three days with the Mandans, trying to persuade a chief to travel with them to Washington to visit President Jefferson. They were unsuccessful because the chiefs were afraid of the Sioux downriver in present-day South Dakota and Nebraska. The leaders then hired René Jessaume, the Frenchman they had met the previous year at the settlement, to act as both interpreter and traveling companion. He was able to talk the Mandan chief, Sheheke, into making the journey, together with his wife and son. Two large canoes were fastened together to accommodate the three Indians plus Jessaume, his Indian wife, son, and daughter.

They made the trip through Sioux country with no problems this time and stopped briefly with the Arikara, who expressed concern for their chief named Ankedouchare, who had gone to St. Louis the previous year with the keelboat crew and had not returned. Unfortunately the chief had fallen ill while in Washington and died there in April, 1806. But the tribe had not yet heard the news. They also held a brief council with the friendly Yankton Sioux, whom they met again at the mouth of the Niobrara. Three days later they visited Floyd's grave on the high hill overlooking the river. They found that Indians had opened it and left it only half-covered. Lewis had sufficiently recovered from his wound to accompany them up the hill and help fill the grave again.

Now the men were really putting muscle to paddle and were traveling as much as eighty miles a day down the broad, silty Missouri. They began meeting more white men and learning more recent national news: Aaron Burr's shooting of Alexander Hamilton in a duel, Captain Zebulon Pike's expedition up the Red and Arkansas Rivers, and the diplomatic problems between the United States and both England and Spain. They also heard the (obviously inaccurate) rumors that their party had been gobbled up by wild animals, wiped out to a man by Indians, and enslaved by the Spaniards.

Medical problems continued. Some of the men suffered from swollen and sore eyes, apparently from the sunlight reflecting off the water. Unable to paddle, they were taken aboard the other canoes. The two extra canoes were set adrift, and the hard paddling continued. That same day, September 20, they saw the first milk cows in more than two years as they passed La Charette. They headed for the bank firing their rifles. A big celebration was held that night and the men had an opportunity to see and touch the first white women they had seen for many, many months. The women probably hadn't received so many appreciative looks and compliments in their lives.

They didn't tarry. At 7:30 A.M. the following day, a Sunday, they climbed back into the canoes and they "plyed thear ores with great desterity" toward St. Louis. People cheered them along the banks and exchanged gunpowder salutes. Finally at noon, September 23, 1806, they pulled into St. Louis. The 7,000-mile, two-year, four-month, and ten-day odyssey was over. The first men to cross the continent by land were home again.

10

Aftermath

Many members of the expedition entered almost immediate obscurity after they returned and except for men such as Colter, life could only be downhill for the average man after such an event. Some of them dropped completely from sight, rumors circulating that they had taken to drink. Others accepted 320-acre plots of land west of the Mississippi granted to them by a grateful Congress in 1807 plus a bonus of double pay. Of these some sold the land and never occupied it, or probably, in some cases, never even saw it.

Some reenlisted in the army, such as Sgts. Gass and Pryor, and Bratton, Shannon, and Willard; perhaps Gibson, Howard, McNeal, and Windsor did, too. Pryor eventually rose to the rank of captain. Some of the others served in the brief War of 1812.

Like Colter, Drouillard went back to the Rockies with Potts, as did Wiser, and possibly Collins. Drouillard was killed by the Blackfeet near Three Forks in 1810; Potts was killed in the same area two years earlier.

After they took Chief Sheheke to Washington, Clark was put in charge of seeing him safely back to his Mandan village. He assigned now-Ensign Pryor to the job and in the summer of 1807, Pryor took a contingent of thirteen men, including Shannon and maybe Gibson, and headed back up the Missouri. When they entered Sioux country, the Indians there were still outraged over the death of their chief, Ankedoucharo. With some allies they attacked Pryor's party, killing four men and wounding nine, including Shannon, who was shot in the leg. Before the party could return to St. Louis, the leg became gangrenous. They stopped at Camp Belle Fontaine, near the mouth of the Missouri above St. Louis, and an Army surgeon amputated it above the knee. Shannon almost died but recovered and went east in 1810 to help Nicholas Biddle decipher and organize the captains' journals for publication. He lived near Lexington, Kentucky for several years and read law there, became a friend of Henry Clay, and served in the Kentucky Legislature. Later he moved to Missouri and became an attorney, state senator, and U.S. attorney before his death in 1838.

On their return, York was not only freed by Clark but also given a six-horse team and wagon, which he used to run a freighting business between Nashville and Richmond. But the venture failed and he began doing odd jobs. When he was apparently on his way to see Clark in St. Louis — the year is unknown — he fell ill of cholera and died. He has no grave.

Sacajawea apparently died in 1812, leaving Little Pomp and another child, a girl named Lizette. Clark became guardian of both children and saw to their education, plus a third Charbonneau issue from another Indian wife, this one Toussaint, a boy.

Charbonneau stayed among the Indians most of his remaining years, and Clark after his appointment as Superintendent of Indian Affairs for the Louisiana Territory, employed him as interpreter. He is known to have visited St. Louis in 1839, and it is believed he died the following year at the age of eighty.

Gass outlived them all and died in 1870 at the age of ninety-nine. Others who lived to a very old age, for that era anyway, were Willard, who was eighty-eight when he died, and Bratton, who died at sixty-three.

The leaders' later years were something of a reflection of the way they lived while on the expedition. Lewis was always something of an unfortunate, accident prone and of a volatile temperament.

First, he was appointed Governor of Louisiana Territory and at the same time Jefferson appointed him to that post, he told him to supervise the publication of a history of the expedition. Lewis wanted his version to be the official one and he was irritated by the plans of some of the enlisted men to publish their versions first. Frazier was the first to announce such plans, but they fell through. Then Gass's version was announced for publication and Lewis denounced it while announcing *his* plans.

When he finally returned to the territory he governed a year after his appointment, he was faced with monumental administrative tasks, in addition to a great deal of hostility from several quarters. Decisions were to be made on licensing traders, settling conflicting land claims, and resolving Indian land and treaty problems, among others. His second-in-command, Frederick Bates, quickly turned against him and caused him a great deal of trouble. Historians have said that had Lewis lived longer, he and Bates undoubtedly would have settled their differences with dueling pistols.

Then he became embroiled with the War Department over a $500 draft he had signed; then another one for $440 was refused. Lewis was furious and decided to go back to Washington to fight it out in person.

When he arrived at Fort Pickering, near present-day Memphis, Tennessee, the post commander found him in such mental anguish that he took Lewis' papers and detained him for a week. He was also told that Lewis' boat crew had been guarding him constantly because he twice had tried to commit suicide.

After being released, Lewis struck out overland instead of

going via ship from New Orleans because, with war between Britain and the United States apparently imminent, he feared he and his papers might fall into British hands. On the night of October 9–10, 1809, Lewis either committed suicide at a roadhouse called Grinder's Stand, near present-day Collinwood, Tennessee, or was killed by highwaymen. There is no way of ever knowing.

The people inside the house were awakened about 3 A.M. by two gunshots, and Lewis was found outside with a bullet wound in his head and another in his chest. According to eyewitnesses, he said, "I have done the business. My good servant give me some water."

If that is an accurate account, Lewis committed suicide. Had it been any other man, there probably would be no doubt in anyone's mind. But we do not let our heroes off so easily. Suicides among them, as with assassinations of presidents and national figures, are not accepted so readily.

By contrast, Clark's later years were happy and fruitful until his death at the age of sixty-nine in 1838. He had served as Superintendent of Indian Affairs continuously and he also was the first governor of the Missouri Territory, a post to which he was reappointed three times. He had the total trust of the Indians with whom he dealt, and they often called on him to negotiate disagreements in person. He was married to Julia Hancock, the sixteen-year-old girl from Fincastle, Virginia, who bore him five children before dying in 1820. He married her cousin a year later, Mrs. Harriet Kennerly Radford, who had three children by her first marriage and then two more by Clark.

He died while visiting his eldest son, Meriwether Lewis Clark. He was buried in what is today Bellefontaine Cemetery in St. Louis, and his funeral procession was a mile long, the largest in the history of St. Louis at the time.

11

The Trail Today

Thousands of people each year use the Lewis and Clark Trail as a general guide for making a vacation in the West, and there are those dedicated historians, both amateur and professional, who make it a point to cover every stretch of mountain, river, and seacoast described by the explorers. It is no wonder: their route traverses some of the most magnificent scenery the nation has to offer. Following it one goes from the wooded bottomlands of the Midwest to the high plains of Nebraska, the Dakotas, and eastern Montana, then into the most dramatic mountain range in North America, down the Columbia River system through gorges to the wild Pacific Coast.

Such a trip has several bonuses for those with the time. Lewis almost reached what is now Glacier National Park, and Clark was close to what became Yellowstone National Park. These make excellent side trips, and an easy detour can also be taken south a bit to the Badlands and Black Hills.

As my family and I found, a month isn't really sufficient to follow the trail thoroughly. One becomes distracted, as we did, with the side trips and later regrets missing a particular stretch of the trail.

It is possible but not really recommended to follow the exact route. The Missouri River has become almost completely slackwater behind the series of dams all the way to Montana. In fact, there is only one stretch of wild river remaining and that is from the Great Falls area to the lake behind Fort Peck Dam. Occasionally one reads of a group planning to retrace the exact route, but it would become so monotonous portaging around the dams and paddling on the lakes that few are attracted to the project.

Instead we found stretches of the route we wanted to follow with some authenticity at a later date. Among them are the wild Missouri from Fort Benton, Montana, down through the magnificent Missouri Breaks to the Fort Peck reservoir, and stretches of the Lochsa and Clearwater Rivers. We wanted to hike over at least a portion of the low Lemhi Pass rather than via the usual four-wheel-drive vehicle. And we would have loved to be able to drift the Yellowstone River instead of drive along it on a four-lane highway.

During that month we found that simply stopping off at all the historic sites connected with the expedition is not necessarily conducive to understanding the expedition. Some, such as Travelers Rest and Canoe Camp are, to be frank, uninteresting. There is no sense of discovery involved while standing elbow-to-elbow with a crowd of people atop Pompey's Pillar. That feeling of discovery, a sharing of the almost mystical experiences imparted by the journals, must come unsolicited. They come on their own and there is no predicting what scene will evoke such moments of illumination, nor are these moments often a class-action emotion. They cannot be shared.

I think the first such moment occurred to me when we drove out of Augusta, Montana, and saw the Rockies far to the west while before us was a twisting dirt track leading from a wire gate that seemed to pull one's eye toward the distant range, where Glacier National Park lies. At the moment I saw that scene, I was struck by the enormity, the audacity, of the expedition. I felt a similar affinity with the explorers again in North Dakota on a cold, rainy afternoon when the gloom obscured the signs of agriculture and turned the landscape into hills rolling off into the distance, much like a stormy sea without breakers. Directly below us was the vast Missouri River. True, it was slackwater but still the feeling was there that no matter what we do to the land, it is going to survive us in one form or another. It is landscape that makes human activity seem terribly trivial.

I would not describe these moments as mystical experiences: I don't think I've ever had one and probably couldn't define one if I had. But at such moments one can appreciate the frustration both Lewis and Clark expressed at mere words trying to describe what lay before their eyes. Their writings were remarkable exercises in descriptive writing. There was almost a cinematic quality to much of their descriptions and after reading the journals, one could watch a silent film of the trip and easily write the subtitles from the journals. This is why, by the way, one sees so many books about the journey with only the explorers' words used for captions and text. The only thing we could add is notes on the location of photographs, paintings, and drawings. They are unique in the annals of exploration and must be judged finally as one of the outstanding endeavors in American literature.

Our trip evolved in a rather round-about fashion. To my astonishment I had been asked to serve on the state of Washington Lewis and Clark Trail Committee at a time when I had neither read their journals nor traveled the trail. Having lived in Seaside, Oregon, and later in Longview, Washington, I was familiar with their activities in those areas, particularly along the coast. I had listened enthralled one afternoon while the late Burnby Bell, historian at Fort Clatsop, told how they had established where the original fort stood by archaeological methods, and I had also watched the late Ted Yates film part of the excellent two-part television special on the explorers. Yates had used some local youths, either Explorer or Sea Scouts, as actors in the film and I remembered how delighted I was that the big Newfoundland dog who portrayed Scannon was not ferocious.

There is a standing joke about travel writers that the best way to find out about an area is to get a book contract on the subject. It forces you to dig rapidly and deeply into research, which explains our month-long trip. We made arrangements for the use of the twenty-seven-foot Itasca motorhome, received a pass to KOA (Kampgrounds of America), and tied the trip in with a visit with relatives in Missouri and made the side trips to Yellowstone and Glacier National Parks.

Just before we left, it occurred to me that we were living at the wrong end of the trail, that it would be best to begin in Missouri and follow the trail with the journals. Or, as a friend slyly remarked, if we insisted on reading the journals as we progressed, we should call the book *Lewis and Clark Through a Rear View Mirror*. He had a point because often during the trip I caught myself looking back to the west when we stopped, trying to visualize the country through their descriptions headed west. So I strongly recommend following the trail in the sequence of the journals.

On the other hand, I have met people who were so afflicted by the Lewis and Clark syndrome that they have traveled the trail several times without seeing, or appreciating, what is there today. Pilgrimages are fine, but one should not ignore the people and places along the way.

Since we live in Washington and lived nearly four years on the Columbia River, we are familiar with the explorers' travels in that part of the country. Hence we abandoned the Columbia River portion, which includes Fort Clatsop and the new interpretative center at Cape Disappointment, and struck out through Washington early that June and drove across the Great Columbia Plain, green and fresh now with young wheat and hay crops, warm but with the heat of July not yet evident.

We had loaded the motorhome in something of a hurry — my wife says I just threw things in, started the motor and honked the horn for them to get in, and then drove off — and consequently we were treated to an assortment of rattles and clinks all the way across the state. We stopped to fill the propane tanks once, then twice, because nobody at the service stations knew exactly how to hook up the hose, and I certainly didn't. Finally we found a professional. He looked at it, guessed correctly it was new, gave it a smart crack with a crescent wrench, and it worked fine.

We planned to pick up the trail at the Snake River and stopped for lunch and a swim at Lyon's Ferry State Park, where the Palouse (Drewyer's River in the journals) enters the Snake. On the way we swung by Palouse Falls State Park, a beautiful waterfall that the explorers barely missed seeing as they explored the deep canyon a short distance from the Snake. But the lower Palouse River and the entire Snake River now comprise a big lake, and sailboats moved slowly back and forth between the canyon walls, silent, stately, and graceful as butterflies. The rapids that caused Lewis and Clark so much grief that fall of 1805 are now nothing more than rocks on the bottom of deep lakes.

We were still in the shakedown stage the second day, still learning how to stack the dishes and pots and pans, and still learning to open cupboard doors ever so slowly where we kept books and games so we wouldn't get thumped on the head by a heavy object. And we were still learning the mysteries of the auxiliary power plant the hard way. Since we live in what boosters call an "air-conditioned climate," we were unfamiliar with amenities such as air conditioning, and we tried to turn on both roof air-conditioners simultaneously. The power plant wasn't equipped for such sudden demands and rebelled by blowing its fuse. Then we read the manual, which explained that power plants are fine pieces of equipment, but they do have limitations. We had to travel several days through the early summer heat before a replacement was air-mailed to us — we didn't exactly have a permanent address at that time — and even when Lewis and Clark were portaging around the Great Falls, being bitten by flies, mosquitoes, and fleas, and having their heads bashed in by hailstones, even then they could not have complained as much as I did.

Although I had been writing for a number of years, it seemed that the quantity and probably the quality of my note-taking diminished with each year to the point that my notes were nothing more than key words to jog my memory later. My first plan was to keep a daily journal and I bought an overpriced notebook for that purpose. But I immediately found several excuses to abandon the plan: no one would want to read my lamentations about the absence of an air conditioner and it embarrassed me to think I was complaining about something as trivial as that; I could not hope to be as interesting as Lewis and Clark even on a good day. Finally our son, who was nine that summer, was keeping a journal that was better than anything I could produce. Sometimes his directness and honesty had the same charm (to a parent who is trying not to be proud) as the Lewis and Clark journals.

It was that last item that reduced my journal to a few pages of virtually useless notes. Diligently, in his careful scrawl, Scott gave a running account of the journey. He took a few days off and when he did, he wrote the real reason, namely, he was bored with the chore. But his first day's entry read:

"May 31, 1975: Today we started on the trail, We had a lot of trouble with the propane tank and the pilot light. At one of the gas stations the tar was melting and I got my foot stuck. We are driving on a road through the woods and there is lots of mountains. We have just entered North Bend (Washington). It's pretty small. While I was writing we went through it. We're back out by the woods. It is very nice out here. My sister was stuck in the bathroom. There is a mountain with a switchback road all the way up. We are in a pass right now. In case you don't know, we are on the way to starting the trail. We have gone by lots of meadows and farms. We're at a store right now and our pilot light is working."

No fancy writing here, and no excuses to cover ignorance of our equipment. Just the facts.

We followed the Snake into the twin cities of Clarkston and Lewiston, drove straight through them and past the lumber mills on the outskirts of Lewiston, then followed the Clearwater on the winding, two-lane highway lined with trees that gave a blinking effect as we drove in and out of the shade, searching for a cool place to camp for the night.

That was also the day we learned a valuable lesson on guide books. We had the AAA guides to all states and some other thick books that listed all campgrounds (supposedly all, at least), and when we saw the signs for Kamp Tomahawk beside the highway, we could not find it listed anywhere. It was a hot day, the children wanted to go swimming, and I wanted the air-conditioner (my lower lip quivers easily), so we pulled into the campground to investigate. A look around convinced us that was the place. It had an elevated swimming pool with rows of movie-theater seats for watching, pens for pheasant and quail, and a "U-fish" pool of trout with a gumball machine filled with fish food so you could pay a nickle, feed the fish, and watch them jump.

A large group of travelers occupied one end of the campground with a variety of recreational vehicles, ranging from a battered and worn school bus to a truck with a plywood box on the back to a relatively new camper-van. There were well over a dozen children in the group, all lively, each of whom knew the words and music to John Denver's hit of the moment, something about being just a plain old country boy. While the whole group sang it *a cappella*, two of the pre-teenage boys danced a shuffling and jumping dance, occasionally toppling off into the pool without missing a beat with their clapping. It was a delightful place to stop, and if the other campers' music failed to interest us, we could always walk across the highway and sit on a sandbar and watch the Clearwater flow swiftly by, rippling and roiling over the rocky bottom, and envy the Lewis and Clark party for *having* to travel this route in boats. It didn't seem like work at all, rather like being paid to have fun.

We were so delighted with the campground that we asked the owner why he wasn't listed in our stack of guidebooks, and he said he didn't need it, didn't need inspectors coming around snooping in his bathrooms, and had told the last AAA inspector to evacuate the premises with as much rapidity as his feet and automobile would provide. He showed the children some quail and pheasant chicks in a makeshift brooder in his office and told them to be careful where they threw the frisbee so they wouldn't fall over a water or sewer connection. Our trip was clearly off to a friendly start.

That evening while taking a shower at the campground, I chatted with a man who was camped there in a small pickup camper with his wife and small daughter. He said he had a good job in Oklahoma and had been living there for several years. But the past winter he and his wife decided they were simply vegetating, worrying about all the things the crab-grass set worries about — the proper furniture, the right kind of patio, the right kind of boat and motor, and all the other emblems of middle-class living. He said his wife was a really good sport and they had just packed it all in. They sold the house and furniture. What they couldn't sell, they either gave away or stored, keeping only the basic equipment they would need when they settled down again. Then they took off.

It had taken them all spring to work their way from Oklahoma to the western Idaho border. Sometimes they stopped in a place for a month if it was friendly, and he usually found himself working somewhere. He knew machinery and he would give a hand to a service station owner or to a farmer. Most of the time he didn't accept pay or if he did, it was very little. His wife would become acquainted with the inhabitants through the church, and they'd always have something to do.

Usually, he said, they'd find a town that didn't have a tourist industry because tourist towns aren't so friendly as others. The past week had been spent in a small Idaho town well off the beaten path, and his usual way of getting acquainted was to find the town marshal, or deputy, or whoever and ask where he could park his camper for a few days. He was never turned away, he said, and sometimes they liked having someone camped around the city park or the public fishing access to keep down vandalism and other forms of nonsense.

How long did they plan to travel? Not much longer, he said. They would probably find a place in Idaho or Oregon before summer ended, then he would get a steady job until they decided to travel again. As some of our friends envied us for our month-long trip, I envied them for their freedom.

We could not hope to duplicate Lewis and Clark's true route through the Bitterroots; only a four-wheel drive vehicle could climb through those mountains over the series of fire roads that more or less follow their route. We had to be content with following the Clearwater, past the canoe camp at Kamiah, then the Lochsa River, up the Lewis and Clark Highway, and over Lolo Pass. The rivers are very pretty streams, very fast and filled with rapids, backwashes, and other hazards to boating. I found myself scouting each set of rapids as we made our numerous stops at the small, cozy campgrounds that dotted the highway. After examining the rivers carefully, I decided the only craft I would take on them would be an inflatable raft. Kayaks are for the younger and more experienced. I can execute half of an Eskimo roll with great skill; it is the second half that panics me.

We traveled this portion of the trail twice and both times felt it was an anticlimax because it is too easy now with the highway, and Lolo Pass itself is, quite simply, very unattractive. Clear-cut patches, like open wounds, were visible from the higher elevations, and we were anxious to get into the higher and boulder-strewn Rockies where there isn't always enough timber to attract the clear-cutters.

The next Lewis and Clark stop would be Lolo Hot Springs, where the much "fortigued" men stopped for warm baths. It is now a popular resort area and the parking lot was jammed with cars near the concrete pool. We proceeded on.

In Missoula, Montana, we pulled into a campground in the middle of a sudden and hard shower that cooled the air to a delightful mid-60s temperature, and we shot the first of perhaps 100 games of pool on the trip in the recreation room. At one time in my youth I thought of myself as a tall Minnesota Fats but shortly afterward I met some real pool players, and I went for years without holding a cue stick. It was with good reason because my wife, who knows as much about pool as I do about needlepoint, walloped me.

It was also in Missoula that we discovered the cultural habits of big campgrounds. They aren't so much places to spend a night as they are to show off your motorhome. It was one big showroom. Our Itasca was introduced that year and we had a steady stream of people walking through and giving forth opinions on its merits and demerits. Some women opened cupboards and the men looked at the engine, checked the power plant, and fiddled with the retractable step. We are privacy lovers, and this was clearly going to take some getting used to. After the Missoula experience we learned to establish visiting hours, which other campers understood and honored. Visiting hours were after dinner at each stop and never in the morning when we were trying to get under way immediately after breakfast.

After visiting hours that night, we pulled down the maps for perhaps the 500th time during the past three months to plot our journey. We had drawn lines on one set of maps so many times that it was illegible and had to go back to AAA for another set. We had settled everything except the route going and coming in the Helena-Missoula-Great Falls area. Lewis and Clark sent so many different groups in so many different directions in that area that we could not possibly hope to follow each route. So we had to decide there if we were going to follow Lewis' route eastward, or Clark's down to the Dillon area for Camp Fortunate. It was almost impossible to decide.

We did what we probably had planned to do all along. We went where we wanted to go and if Lewis and Clark's footsteps crossed the highway ahead of us, so much the better. We wanted to take side trips to two places they almost but not quite found: Yellowstone National Park and Glacier National Park. We chose the latter for our first expedition and in the process hoped to see the Gates of the Mountains, then go near, at least, Lewis and Clark Pass between Missoula and Great Falls, Camp Disappointment where Lewis ended his Marias exploration, and the Great Falls. If we could throw in a boat trip through Gates of the Mountains and the Missouri Breaks, so much the better.

We drove toward Helena the next morning and after we were nearly there, I realized I had made my first blunder on the Lewis and Clark route. Our journal-keeping son and navigator pointed out that we were on the wrong highway. The exact, or nearly exact, route would be over Highway 200 to Great Falls but we were on Highway 12, which led over McDonald Pass and then down to Helena. I glared at him as chagrined parents are wont to do, grew stubborn, refused to backtrack, and drove on into Helena. My first thought was that nobody would know the difference, but no parent has yet learned how to make children keep family secrets. So I had to tell them it was impossible to follow the exact route because Lewis and Clark Pass is on a forest service road too rough and steep to take the motorhome. That part was true, but they knew it wasn't the whole reason. "Daddy got lost," was the more accurate verdict.

Helena sits in a broad valley with rolling plains that lead upward to mountains on three sides, one of the most beautiful places to build a city we have seen. My wife is a native Washingtonian and has found few places in our travels that compare favorably with her home state. The next morning when we went out to explore Helena and saw the mountains all around the cuplike valley, she said she thought she might be able to tolerate Montana if forced to leave the coast.

We were still in the shakedown stage of the journey and trying to get our sleeping arrangements organized. We bought a set of washable sleeping bags for the trip, and the three girls wanted the almost kingsized bed in the rear to themselves. My wife and

I are both tall, so we took the double bed that comes from the cafe seats and the swing-down bunk above the driver's compartment. That left the son without a place of his own, other than the floor, which he thought would be a great place to sleep.

His June 3 journal entry explains the day and its problems clearly:

"We kept finding letters on mountains. We are at a KOA. The pinball machine was broken and it kept giving you games. The sleeping on the floor doesn't work out right. I get in the way. We bought a bunch of tapes for our tape player. We drove one hundred and thirteen miles."

No, his sleeping on the floor didn't work out. He was stepped on several times, and his bellows of pain and rage were so loud that his sisters gladly shared the rear bed with him for the duration of the trip.

The following day we drove north toward Gates of the Mountain, hoping to take the boat ride through the slackwaters of the canyon but found we would have at least a two-hour wait. Instead, we decided to drive on toward Camp Disappointment and try the boat ride on the return trip. We cut across the rolling landscape on Highway 287 through Augusta and Choteau, past herds of cattle spotted on the land where once buffalo grazed, across bridges over dry gullies too narrow for both a motorhome and a motorcycle at the same time, it seemed, and on north toward Glacier National Park. It was early in the season for mountain travel and we had been warned that the Going-To-The-Sun Highway, which bisects the park, might still be closed. When we pulled in at the KOA at St. Mary, near the park entrance, we found that, indeed, the snow was still too deep to open the highway more than about fifteen miles on the east side.

After we parked and began doing the laundry, the wind came up strong and steady, dry as a desert wind. And the static electricity started jumping, sometimes an inch from the finger to metal. We could hear it popping and snapping as people forgot to ground themselves. For the first time since we became parents, our children could make us cower in fright simply by pointing a finger at us. We knew mischief was in the making when the children scuffed their feet on the nylon carpet with an angelic look on their faces.

The wind increased after dark, blowing down off the mountains of the park and rocking the motorhome. I walked up to the office to mail a letter and found the owner ready to close for the night. I asked him if that much wind was unusual and he shrugged and said it often was worse. By this time, he said, it was hitting about sixty miles per hour in gusts and steadying at around forty. I bought a small book about the park and went back to the motorhome. The book told us that 100-mile-an-hour winds were not uncommon. We didn't doubt it. Later that night we heard several of the other motorhomes and campers starting up engines and milling around. I looked outside and saw that nearly everyone else had unhooked themselves from the electricity and water and were turning to point into the wind like a herd of cows in a storm. We decided to sit it out and were rocked to sleep.

It was still spring in the high country and the valley floors were a bright, almost damp, green and sprinkled with wildflowers. We saw vast fields of flowers as we drove into the park, and we stopped a few miles up the Going-To-The-Sun Highway to stare back at a group of five or six bighorn sheep standing on a snowbank beside the highway, their coats long and dirty, apparently from rolling in the dust.

We drove to Browning, in the heart of the Blackfeet reservation, and stopped at the Museum of the Plains Indians. Like so many federal museums, there was a lot of floor space with mediocre exhibits. It had a generally sterile appearance and we left, no more educated about the Blackfeet Indians than when we entered. It left the impression that the exhibits were put together in a manner that could not possibly offend anyone, with the result that nothing was said.

We would have liked to visit the small grove of trees that mark Camp Disappointment, but that would involve traipsing across private land. Instead, we drove east on Highway 2, then turned north on Highway 444 toward the Canadian border until we reached Cut Bank Creek. By driving a few yards beyond the bridge we could see, across a cultivated field with a pile of junk in the middle, the grove of trees at Camp Disappointment. We paused briefly beside the highway to try (unsuccessfully) to take a photograph of the site. As we drove off, the inevitable conversation with one of our daughters ensued:

"What was that place?"

"Camp Disappointment."

"Sure was."

I was reminded of one of my favorite Dennis the Menace cartoons in which Dennis sat with his parents at a candle-lit table, and Dennis said, "I don't think it's romantic. I think it's dark." Children are pragmatic and realistic, and any attempt to tell them how important the Lewis and Clark expedition was to the course of American history sounds suspiciously like school at its worst. We satisfied ourselves by telling them of the expedition as briefly as possible, mentioning certain exciting things that happened at specific places along our route and let them ask the questions. Our hope was that they would learn by a process of osmosis. Later conversations with them indicate they absorbed much more history than we expected.

As they have entered their teens and made friends who have a habit of zipping off to France and Switzerland and Italy for the summer, they have repeatedly asked us why we don't travel to Europe and Asia. A trip across the West is nice, they say, but a trip to Europe would be "cool." Our trip along the Lewis and Clark trail is the best answer I can give. Given my personal choices, I will travel in my own country first for the simple reason that I want to see every nook and cranny it has to offer and to talk to its people. Traveling to other countries gives perspective; traveling in my own country fertilizes my cultural and emotional roots.

We drove out to the Great Falls and then on to Giant Springs. The falls, of course, have been virtually demolished by the dams that are strung along the river in the area, and one must dig into historical photographic files and read Lewis' and Clark's descriptions of them to appreciate their drama before the dams. We did not tarry long at them.

But we found Giant Spring State Park a very pleasant place to visit, and the fascination a river can create is multiplied by watching water rumble out of the earth at a regular pace, day after day, century after century. The explorers guessed, with some accuracy, that the spring increases the river's flow by nearly one-fourth. It is a phenomenal amount of water that pours out of the spring and a cool, green, and shady place to visit.

After Great Falls, we drove south again to pick up the other near-miss by the explorers, Yellowstone, and at the same time follow the Missouri River as far as we could toward its headwaters. We stopped on the outskirts of Helena to buy gasoline and as soon as our order was taken, the owner of the service station insisted, almost demanded, that all six of us get out, come in, and sit a spell. We did, and he served my wife and me coffee and gave the children some fruit punch. He asked where we were going, then said he wasn't being nosy, just wanted to be sure we knew the snow was still too low in Glacier National Park for much driving and to recommend that we go into the park from the west side "because it is a lot prettier." He said his station was one of the best locations in Helena, on the eastern edge of town where several streets and two highways converge, and that he was in the gasoline business because he liked to meet new people, not to get rich. Anyone going into that business to get rich has an unpleasant surprise in store, he said. When we told him where we were going, he told us to watch for herds of antelope out on Highway 287 near Winston. We did, and he was right. The beautiful, fleet animals were in small bunches across a long, open hillside that sloped up from the highway.

When we reached Three Forks, we pulled in at the KOA campground only six days after the camping season opened throughout most of Montana. This KOA sat on a high hill overlooking the Three Forks town and valley and it was so new that the swimming pool wasn't completed yet. Most people were still home because school wasn't out yet, and the owner apologized for not having a place for the children to swim but told us of a good swimming hole the other side of town, equipped with a float and diving board and, as we were to find out, a gorgeous sunset while we cooked dinner on a charcoal pit.

One almost needs an airplane to appreciate the Three Forks area because each of the three rivers looks very much alike from the highway, through no fault of man's. When we went out to the Three Forks Visitor Center — a stone-and-concrete shelter with metal maps showing the rivers — we decided to have breakfast at the park. The mosquitoes that plagued Lewis and Clark had multiplied and they shared our breakfast. We took our revenge, quite unintentionally, when they did their suicidal stunt of landing on a spoonful of cereal just as it entered one of the six mouths. Some breakfasts on that trip were finished sooner than others.

From Three Forks south to Dillon, the fun of following the trail finally appeared. Many of the landmarks Lewis and Clark had mentioned were either gone or buried under dam backwaters, but from Three Forks on we began watching for Beaverhead Rock, knew exactly what it looked like, and felt a sense of discovery when we drove past it. We sympathized with the earlier explorers when we drove across bridges over the

Beaverhead River because in spots it didn't look deep enough to float a modern canoe and certainly not one of the deep-draught wooden dugouts they had used. Clark's stubborn determination to get the canoes up this valley must have caused a great deal of muttering among the troops as they heaved and strained against the "toeroaps."

After visiting Camp Fortunate, or at least the lake that covers it, we drove on to Yellowstone, which impressed Scott:

"June 8, 1975: We have got to Yellowstone and Old Faithful is closed. The road is under nine feet of snow. We are at a KOA. We visited a place where the 1959 earthquake struck. It was very torn up. One of the highways was gone in earthquake lake. The place that we are staying at has a neat playground. A little girl was sitting on the merry-go-round and she went flying off and broke her glasses.

"June 9, 1975: Today we went to Yellowstone. It was more than I expected. Old Faithful wasn't as much as you think. It goes about eighty feet in the air. It only stays high about fifty seconds. The place that it is in has lots of geysers, thermal pools, fumeroles, and mud geysers. We saw Morning Glory Pool. It's very colorful and deep. It looks like it goes down to the center of the earth. At a gas station the man didn't put our gas cap back so we had to come back after we were through with driving for the day. We filled up on propane and it took five seconds for eight gallons to get in it. The man was so cautious that he made everyone get out."

We caught the trail again at Livingston and followed Clark's route back to the Missouri River. We had to give up our hope of making a float trip down the Missouri Breaks from Fort Benton, and there was virtually no way we could follow the Missouri otherwise. The highways avoid it and only an occasional secondary road cuts across the badlands to dead-end at the river and later at the vast lake behind Fort Peck Dam. That stretch of the trail, so important and so beautiful, is one we will have to travel later.

For the next three days we continued on along the Yellowstone River, first losing elevation steadily from nearly 5,000 feet around Livingston, then gaining again in the High Plains to 2,000 feet at Williston, North Dakota. We stopped at a campground that featured horseback rides, and the children got their first view of a prairie dog town and saw their first loco weed, which the wrangler said worked on animals the way marijuana works on people. That they understood, but only, I hope, from schoolyard conversations.

And we stopped off at Pompey's Pillar to climb it and paused to read Clark's signature and date, now covered with a piece of thick glass. A marker told us that Custer had camped there once, and we wondered where the Blackfeet Indians were when American history needed them.

We stopped for gas in Sidney, Montana, and since no map in our possession gave a number to the highway leading north and across the Missouri River to Forts Union and Buford, we asked the service station attendant for directions. He was a pleasant young man, perhaps a senior in high school, and he looked puzzled when I told him what we were looking for. Then I could see recognition light up his eyes, and then they clouded over again. He said he hated to tell us, but he had been all over the Dakotas, Montana, and even out to the Coast but never in his entire life had he ever driven north of town to the historic sites. Kept meaning to, he said, but just never got around to it. He went inside and came back out a few minutes later and told us how to reach the still unnumbered highway and said there were signs showing the way.

At first I thought it odd that one can live in a place that long and never visit such well-known places, but my wife pointed out that I had lived in Washington State nearly as long as the young service station attendant had been on this earth and had never been to Lopez Island, only a short distance from Seattle. She had me there. It must prove the truth of the adage that if you want directions, ask another tourist, not a native.

We drove out the highway, followed the signs, turned on a gravel road that soon became a dirt road along the edges of some farms, and finally came to a halt at a bridge. The highway, or road, at this point was going in one direction, but the bridge pointed at right angles to the road. At the end of the bridge was a traffic light with the red signal on above a sign. The sign explained the operation of the railroad bridge. The light operated, if I remember correctly, at seven-minute intervals. The bridge was so narrow (the railroad shared it with the highway) that two cars could not meet on it without one of them backing off. Our wait wasn't long, and we were permitted to go across the tall structure. It undoubtedly was the tallest and skinniest bridge any of us had ever seen and when we were across, we stopped to look it over more closely. It was a drawbridge, and the mecha-

Railroad-highway bridge near Fort Union site

nism appeared to be intact but rusted so badly that it would take a crew of men armed with drums of liquid wrench to put it in working order. We asked about the bridge later and found that it was owned by the Burlington Northern Railroad and was built when steamboats were still trying to navigate the Missouri. They ran up and down the river for a number of years, but it was always an ulcer-making chore because the channel wandered so much and the water was so full of deadheads and sawyers. Our informant also said the bridge was built on the tail end of the steamboat years, and to his knowledge the drawspan had been used only twice. I liked his version of the bridge story so much that I didn't pry further. Somebody was liable to make the story dull. I like my history accurate, but I also like good stories.

We drove down the Missouri a few miles on a road so rough that we expected at almost any minute to find it dead-ending in some rancher's corral. But it continued on until we saw a tall flagpole seemingly in the middle of nowhere, then some mobile homes, and finally a sign stating that we were at Fort Union, a national historic site.

Immediately after we parked, a young ranger emerged from one of the buildings and offered to take us on a guided tour. We were intrigued because there didn't seem to be anything to tour, other than a broad space on the knoll overlooking the river. Also, he had a delightful North Carolina accent and living as we do in a place where nearly everyone speaks Hollywood English, we thought it would be interesting for the children to hear the young man's speech. They said later it was only the second time they had ever spoken directly to someone with a southern accent. They had been exposed from birth to a variety of European and Asian accents but to none of the regional accents of our own country. Clearly they were culturally deprived.

The ranger told us a brief history of the fort, of how it was built as a trading post for the American Fur Company in 1829. He said it took the traders four years to complete it to the satisfaction of the factor, Kenneth McKenzie. He had a wall 220 feet long built of thick cottonwood trees and the posts were twenty feet high with stone bastions at each corner and foundations of stone. It had a roomy, gracious house for the "bourgeoisie" with a planked exterior painted white with green trim. The interior was papered and well furnished and served as a mess hall and office. Three black cooks worked in a separate kitchen.

The post lasted until 1865, when the trading company was sold by Pierre Chouteau to the North-west Fur Company. It was abandoned a short time later and scavenged by the Army for building materials for Fort Buford a short distance downstream.

The ranger said the major work done so far was strictly archaeological to establish the perimeters of the post and buildings and that maybe, Congress permitting, the post would be reconstructed some day.

He watched the way we stepped, paused, then stepped, and told us there was little danger of rattlesnakes around the post. Besides, he assured us, the prairie rattlers were "shy." He said that, for some reason, his home state of North Carolina led the nation in snakebites and death from poisonous snakes, adding that he wasn't certain if that meant there were more poisonous snakes there, or if it was simply a commentary of some kind about North Carolinians. Since we are from an area with no poisonous snakes and have traveled in the North where there are virtually no snakes of any kind, we have an exaggerated fear of them. One of our daughters is a great lover of wildlife, and we were certain that she could pick up a rattler, pet it, and never feel the fang. Until one of us screamed and fainted, of course.

Only a short distance down the river and on the same road is Fort Buford, which has been accorded state — but not yet national — historic site status. Only two buildings remain of the once important fort, the officer's headquarters and the powder magazine. The parade ground and all the rest is now farmland.

The officer's headquarters is a museum with a fascinating collection of military hardware from a century ago — rifles, swords, uniforms, saddles, photographs, Indian artifacts, and so forth. It was built in 1866 as a control point in the illegal traffic of arms and liquor among the Assiniboin, Crow, Sioux, and Cree Indians. The Indians were no happier at its construction than the bootleggers among the whites, and the Sioux especially were bad about raids against the soldiers who ventured from the post. It was there that the Nez Percé leader, Chief Joseph, was imprisoned after his long running battle was lost, and Chief Sitting Bull surrendered there in 1881. The fort was finally abandoned in 1895 and the buildings were sold at public auction.

Our next stop, which we had passed enroute to Fort Buford, was a small park with a broad, grassy lawn at the confluence of the Yellowstone and the Missouri Rivers. We parked and got out to let the children play on the swings and merry-go-round while I looked for the Yellowstone across the brown Missouri. It all looked alike. We could no more see the Yellowstone than we could the Columbia. It was all big muddy water from where we stood. Oh well, we shrugged, we're here. Let's eat lunch.

Then schedules, one of civilization's worst self-inflicted blights, caught up with us. We still had many points of interest to see, but we were almost at the Canadian border and I had promised my relatives we would be in southern Missouri on a specific day. They were making arrangements for time off from work to meet us, and it undoubtedly would have cast a pall over the gathering had we arrived two or three days late. So we started driving late in the afternoon with no particular goal in mind so long as it was to the south.

We drove across the rich North Dakota farm country with the neat piles of stones dotting the fields like Indian post offices on the Lolo Trail when Lewis and Clark crossed it, and we wondered what significance archaeologists would give them in centuries to come. Would they say they were religious offerings? Territorial boundaries? Whatever, for the time being, the farmers know only that they won't be tearing up machinery on those particular rocks and whenever they have a backache in their declining years, they can blame it on picking up those blasted rocks.

It was almost dark and the sky threatened rain so we took the first campground we could find, which was across Lake Sakakawea from New Town at an Indian-owned resort. It took us some time to adjust to the Dakota spelling and pronunciation of the name of Charbonneau's wife but we weren't going to get into that old argument with anyone. What difference does it make? We're all talking about the same lady. She could neither read nor write, and her people never worried about birth certificates and drivers' licenses. If she couldn't spell her own name, why should we get so excited? But the controversy still rages among Lewis and Clark scholars.

We drove across Four Bears Bridge, a high span over the backwaters of the Missouri behind Garrison Dam, and went into the Four Bears Recreation Area Resort complex. There is a combination hotel, conference center, and campground all together, plus a museum that we were told was excellent, but it was closed during our stay. When we checked in, I saw a sign stating that the pool was for the exclusive use of guests registered at the hotel. Nothing was said about us campground users. I thought perhaps there was another pool for us, but no, there was only the big — and very chilly — lake. So I walked back up to the hotel and asked the friendly young Indian woman at the counter if the sign meant we could not swim in the indoor, heated pool. She gave me a sly grin and asked what sign. We had the big pool to ourselves.

The bridge intrigued us and we asked about the Four Bears name. The woman at the desk gave us some literature and told us to be sure and read about the naming of the bridge. We did and found that not only did the bridge have another name, it had nineteen of them! There was another bridge at the same place before the Garrison Dam was built, and it was dedicated in 1933. It was going to be named for a famous Mandan chief whose portrait was painted several times in the 1830s by George Catlin. But there was another chief across the way, a Hidatsa, also named Four Bears, who had died a few years before the bridge came into being. In an effort to keep peace the original bridge, which pointed north and south, was named at either end for a different Four Bears.

When the new bridge was built, a much higher and longer one that points east and west, the names stayed. But the Mandans appointed a group of associate chiefs to be added to the bridge's name. They were Charging Eagle, Red Buffalo Cow, Flying Eagle, Black Eagle, and Waterchief. The Hidatsas appointed Poor Wolf, Porcupine, Crow Paunch, Big Brace, Crow-Flies-High, Big Hawk, and Old Dog. The third tribe involved, the Arikaras, wanted a piece of immortality, too, and they appointed Bear Chief, Son-Of-The-Star, White Shield, Peter Beauchamp, Sr., and Bobtail Bull. So the bridge with nineteen names is still called Four Bears. I think I know why.

One more major stop in North Dakota and then south with haste, I told the family the next morning. We had been around Fort Clatsop many times and I had covered the filming of an NBC-TV special on Lewis and Clark when the crew arrived there in their buckskins, carrying muskets and accompanied by a dog to represent Scannon. But little, if anything, had been said about Fort Mandan. We wondered why it had not been reconstructed and turned into a major interpretative center as Fort Clatsop had been. We saw on a state map a place called Fort Mandan, on the east side of the Missouri River and upstream a few miles from Washburn.

It was easy to find and we were glad we went. Since the Missouri had changed its channel a short time after the explorers were there, the original fort site was somewhere in the middle of the river. But the McLean County Historical Society had undertaken the project in 1969 and, through a fund-raising drive and with volunteer labor, had built a fort as close to the original as possible by reading carpenter-Sgt. Gass's journals. The rounded triangular fort is rough hewn, much as the original must have been, and sits on a broad, sandy shelf near the river's edge. After visiting it, we walked to the river because it was the first time we had seen the Missouri flowing since leaving Montana. The river was slowly cutting into the bank beneath our feet and we feared for the future of the new fort. We hoped that purists in the National Park Service and elsewhere would not refuse assistance in creating a fort as interesting in North Dakota as they had in Oregon.

We stayed in a beautiful campground high on a hill above Bismarck that night and, while the rain beat on the roof, talked to the campground owner about the days before dams on the Missouri when floods were apparently a common occurrence in Bismarck. It was not an event people anticipated in the same way they do a Fourth of July picnic. This clearly was not a place to expound any theories of leaving Mother Nature alone.

It had rained so much that spring that a good portion of North Dakota was in lakes, and it rained all the next day as we drove due south on Highway 83, an almost straight line that would take us to Pierre, South Dakota by late afternoon. We felt very cozy inside the quiet motorhome with the rain falling in sheets outside and when we stopped for gas at a small town — I believe it was Linton — the people gathered around the service station were so friendly that I regretted not being able to spend an hour drinking a soft drink and talking with them.

We proceeded on our way. We drove straight through Pierre, then climbed up on top of the rolling hills beyond Bad Humoured Island and the Bad River, and immediately the description by Lewis quoted earlier about this part of the country came back to me. The rain had stopped and a long, winding cloud formation led almost from horizon to horizon, passing directly over our heads. I hunted frantically for a place to pull to the side of the road so I could stop and use some film, hoping to capture that after-the-rain look of the rough, steep hills with a touch of sunlight catching the water on the grass, and with the sky gradually darkening toward the southeast. I finally stopped on the narrow shoulder, turned on the blinkers, and ran across the road to take that immortal photograph. I took two cameras, one for black-and-white and the other for color, and used nearly half a roll of each. When we returned home and had the film processed, I had a rather nice picture or two. That was all. The beauty of that moment was one that could only be experienced, never shared.

Three events remain in our minds of the rest of the eastward-bound trip, and only one of those is related to Lewis and Clark. Perhaps it was our love of mountains that colored our thinking but it seemed the closer we got to the Midwest, the more remote the adventure became.

The first event was nothing particularly exciting or unique, but we enjoyed it as one of those pleasant moments of the trip. We wanted to stick with the Missouri River as closely as possible, and drove from a totally unremarkable campground on Interstate Highway 90 down a series of secondary highways to

Drinking Water, South Dakota, directly across the river from Niobrara, Nebraska. We saw, in tiny print on the maps, that a ferry crosses the river there. We are suckers for ferries, no matter where they are, no matter how rickety or even unnecessary they are to our trip plans.

When we arrived at the ferry landing, it was one of those places where you'd better have good brakes or be adept at climbing out of sinking vehicles. The ferry was on the Nebraska side when we arrived, so the children had time to raid our entertainment budget for quarters and then go outside to support whoever owned the soft-drink machines in a little shelter by the dock. There was no ticket window, no office, just a sign that gave the prices for various vehicles.

When the ferry began its return journey, we saw that it had a truck camper on it, a few foot passengers, and no other vehicles. There was a line behind us, and a line on the far side. Apparently patience is one of the virtues of the ferry customer.

When the ferry pulled in to land, I was certain the boatman was going to give us the news that we were too big for his vessel. It looked very, very small and our motorhome looked very, very large and long. And he loaded vehicles crosswise on the deck rather than lengthwise. But he waved us on with no sign of alarm or concern and following his instructions, I drove forward until I could look straight down into the muddy, cold-looking Missouri River. Then he told me to stop. We got off and the twenty-seven foot motorhome was hanging over both sides of the ferry. It looked like a backpacker carrying a baby grand. As we crossed the river, a motorboat came downstream close to the far bank and while we watched it, we could tell the exact moment the operator saw the motorhome on the ferry. The boat lurched to the side, straightened up, then made a right-angle turn to follow and have a closer look at us. He pulled alongside, stared a moment, shook his head in disbelief, and then roared away. We solemnly waved goodbye.

The next two incidents both occurred in Sioux City, Iowa. When we stopped that night on the north end of town at a campground, we noticed that one of the front tires was badly worn and out of alignment. Apparently it had happened the previous day while we were wandering around on the country roads in North Dakota, looking at forts. We had to have it fixed the next day. Through a series of telephone calls we found a shop that might be able to align the wheels. We called them and they told us they couldn't handle trucks but another place could, and they gave us the number. We made an appointment with the spring-and-tire dealer for early afternoon, and then left the campground for a look around. The engine began to gulp and lurch, and I wondered if we would be able to reach the top of the hill of an off-ramp on the freeway. So I called the first garage again and told them we had a new problem. Bring it right in, they said.

I told my wife what I'd just heard on the telephone and neither of us believed it. Nobody, but nobody, just drives into a big garage and gets worked on immediately. But we fumbled around the series of one-way streets until we found the place. They pulled some cars out of the way, then the foreman drove the motorhome into the tiny space and listened to the engine for a couple of minutes. Then he told us he thought an engine tune-up would get us on our way again.

We hadn't had breakfast yet so he sent us up the street and over a block to one of those cafes that exists only in our memories of better times. They were accustomed to serving men who worked with their muscles, and their helpings were gigantic. The waitress gave the children more than they could eat, free refills of milk, and when one of the girls finished her orange juice, a man sitting near her told the waitress she needed another shot. The waitress laughed and "filled 'er up" again. The bill was so low it looked like we'd been given a discount. I overtipped and everyone in the place told the children goodbye.

Back over at the garage they were almost through with the tune-up and the foreman was perplexed. He said he thought the tune-up had solved the problem, but he had a feeling he was overlooking something. It was one of those things he couldn't put his finger on and it bothered him. He asked if we were coming back through on our way home and said if we were and the vehicle still wasn't running right, to drop in and he'd have another look at it. As it turned out he had overlooked something, but it took three more stops before a mechanic in Kansas City found it: the fuel filter was plugged with grass and leaves.

I mention this because it is significant of the whole trip, all the way across the West and back. Whenever we had a problem with the motorhome, we invariably were taken care of immediately. My wife jokingly suggested that all we needed to do was drive into a garage, turn the children loose among the tools, and they'd do anything to get us out in a hurry. But that was only a

Sergeant Floyd's monument, Sioux City, Iowa

joke because the mechanics were simply helpful. We obviously were on vacation and several of them commented that nobody wanted to spend a vacation sitting around waiting for repairs.

Although it was late in the day before we left Sioux City, we decided to pay our respects to Sgt. Floyd on our way out of town rather than take the chance that we might change our route or drive through at night on our return trip. The people of Sioux City have taken good care of the sergeant's memorial, and we were again impressed when we did not expect to be. The miniature Washington's monument standing on the high hill overlooking the Missouri is simple, dramatic, and in excellent taste. There is no hint of commercialism about Sioux City's gesture to the Lewis and Clark party's single casualty.

By now this struck us as a little unusual. We had long become accustomed to seeing everything from motels, hotels, hot dog stands, real estate agencies, and automobile dealers named for the explorers. It is a talisman for western businessmen and a convenience for those who cannot dream up a name of their own. Below Sioux City the Missouri River loses nearly all its remaining charm and becomes less and less a river. Instead, it is something of a liquid highway. So we gave up our diligent route tracing and drove directly south to visit my family.

On the return trip we ignored the trail and went through the Black Hills, across the top of Wyoming and through Yellowstone briefly, enroute to the trail again where it meets the highway near Salmon, Idaho. Then we followed the Lewis and Clark route back to Lolo Pass, going over it and down the Clearwater and so home again. As we had done with Lewis and Clark Pass, we bypassed Lemhi Pass because we did not have the proper vehicle for climbing over steep, rutted tracks that can demolish a highway vehicle.

But there was one more incident that traveling families will recognize as a hazard of long trips and one which must have occurred at various intervals during the trip in 1804–06.

We had prided ourselves on how well the family got along but when we reached Yellowstone again, we had a problem. Everyone was tired from three or four long days of simply trying to add up the miles. Each of us wanted to get home and the bickering increased. I thought the girls were ganging up on the navigator and journal-keeper and told them so. It continued and finally I lost control. I pulled to the side of the road near a herd of elk grazing calmly, and I started to rant and rave. I told them we were going straight home from Yellowstone and we were skipping the Salmon sidetrip. I told them we were going to arrive home two days early. I told them this particular family might never go on another long trip. I told them we were going to drive all night. I told them to forget about our plans to visit the Black Hills some future summer. I told them . . . well, lots of things, I was a little upset.

Scott, over whom the incident occurred, had the last word. My wife and I read it long after the trip in his journal, one of his last entries:

"June 27: Today we went through Yellowstone and our Dad got mad at us and stopped and was saying that we wouldn't go to Salmon and we ended up going to Salmon. We are staying at a KOA and it doesn't have a pool but it has two pool tables and that junk. I was coming from the shower and thought I heard something so I looked around and took off for the rig."

I got the distinct feeling that getting scared in the dark beside the Salmon River was more interesting, and satisfying to remember, than having a parent butt in on his squabbles with his sisters. And as I write this, we have been discussing a trip to the Black Hills.

It made me wonder how many members of the Lewis and Clark Expedition, irritated at one of the leaders, and themselves for not staying home, swore they'd never again leave the woods of Kentucky and Missouri. But they, too, went on other treks across the West.

Introduction To The Maps

In 1975 the Bureau of Outdoor Recreation, Mid-Continent Region, issued an environmental impact statement for the proposed Lewis and Clark National Historic Trail, 3,700 miles of urban areas, farmlands, river bottoms, wilderness, and sea coast. Such a project has been the dream of many Lewis and Clark students for more than a century now, and the proposal is before Congress at this writing.

The following maps are taken from the environmental impact statement, with only a few minor changes to update the information, and to place emphasis on historic sites and monuments along the route. State historical societies and other interested parties have located nearly all compsites the expedition used along the route, but there are obviously too many to include in a book of this nature.

Instead, the recreational opportunities along the route are given emphasis to encourage people to travel the route so they can not only appreciate the hardships the members of the Lewis and Clark expedition experienced and the natural beauty they saw, but also understand more deeply why many consider the expedition the single most important event in the westward expansion of this country.

Sites of interest along the route of Lewis and Clark are indicated by numbers on the maps corresponding to the numbers in the key immediately following the maps. Sites directly related to the Lewis and Clark expedition are in italic type.

The route of the Lewis and Clark expedition

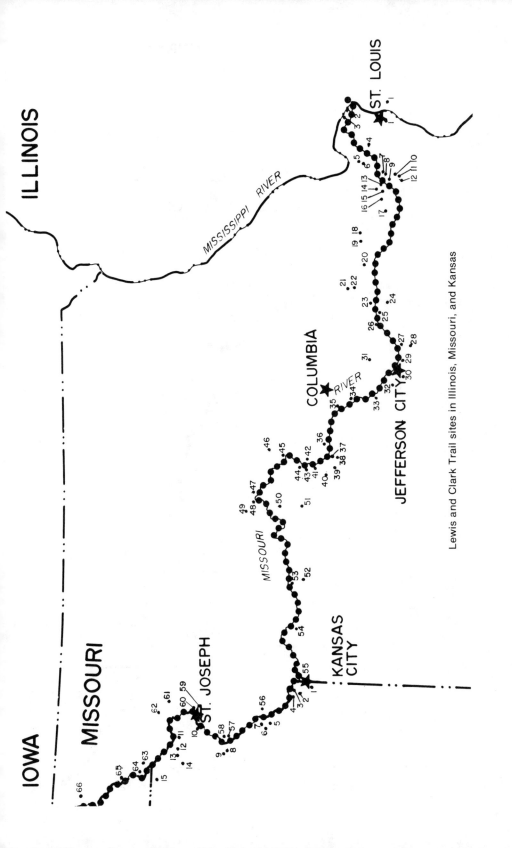

Lewis and Clark Trail sites in Illinois, Missouri, and Kansas

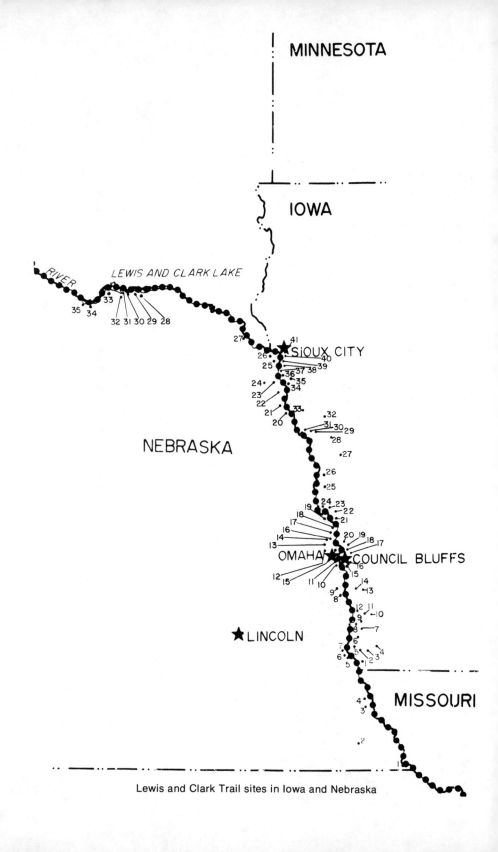

Lewis and Clark Trail sites in Iowa and Nebraska

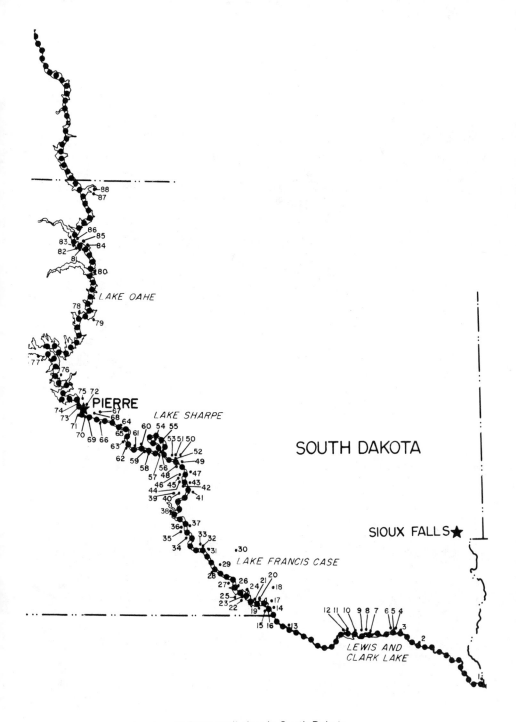

Lewis and Clark Trail sites in South Dakota

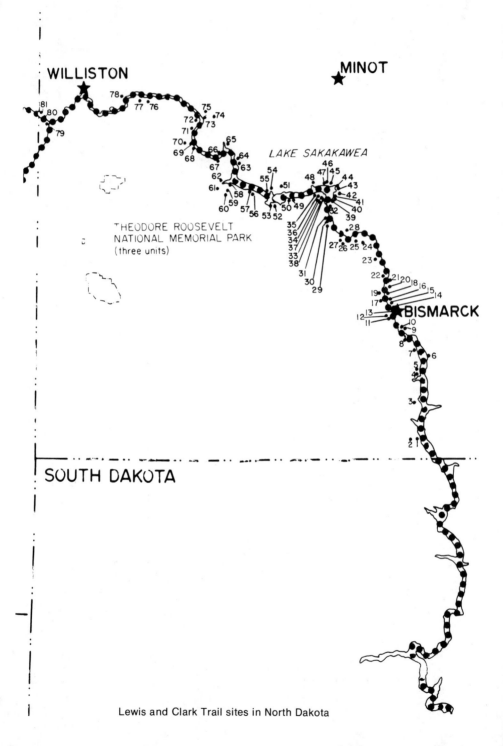

Lewis and Clark Trail sites in North Dakota

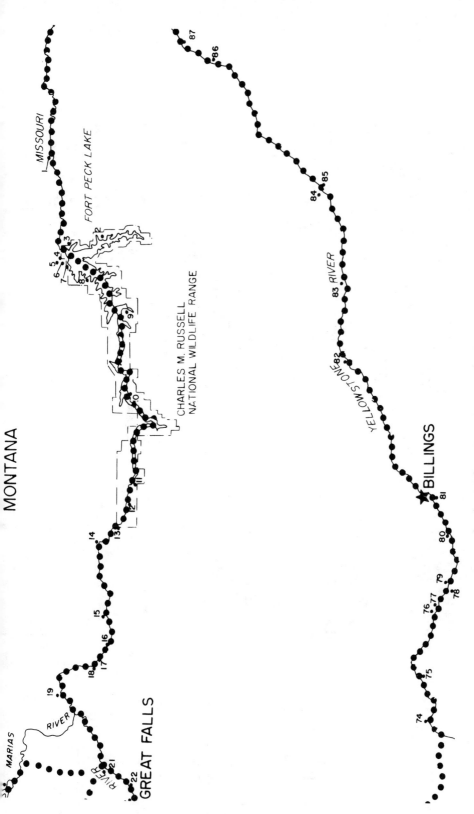

MONTANA

MISSOURI

FORT PECK LAKE

CHARLES M. RUSSELL
NATIONAL WILDLIFE RANGE

MARIAS

RIVER

GREAT FALLS

RIVER

YELLOWSTONE

RIVER

BILLINGS

Lewis and Clark Trail sites in Montana, nos. 1-22 and 74-87

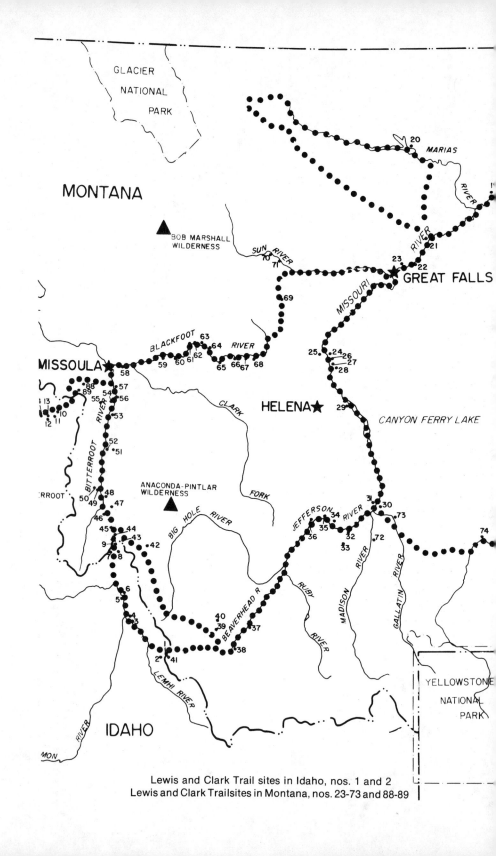

Lewis and Clark Trail sites in Idaho, nos. 1 and 2
Lewis and Clark Trailsites in Montana, nos. 23-73 and 88-89

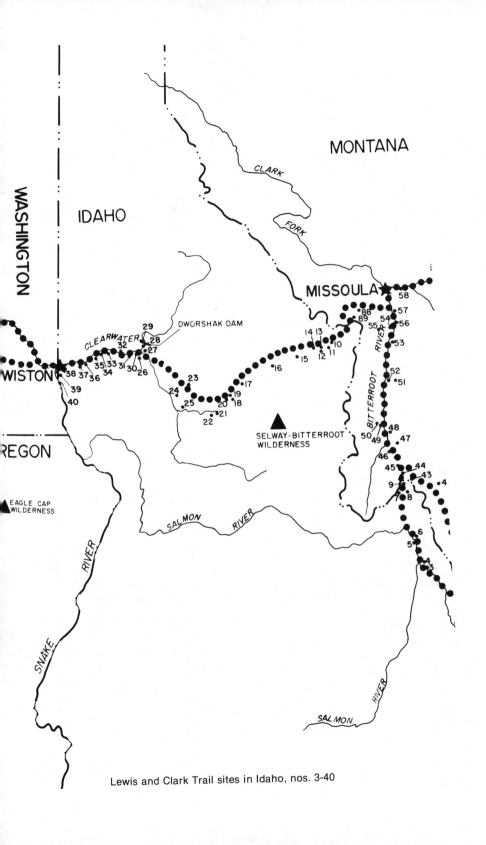

Lewis and Clark Trail sites in Idaho, nos. 3-40

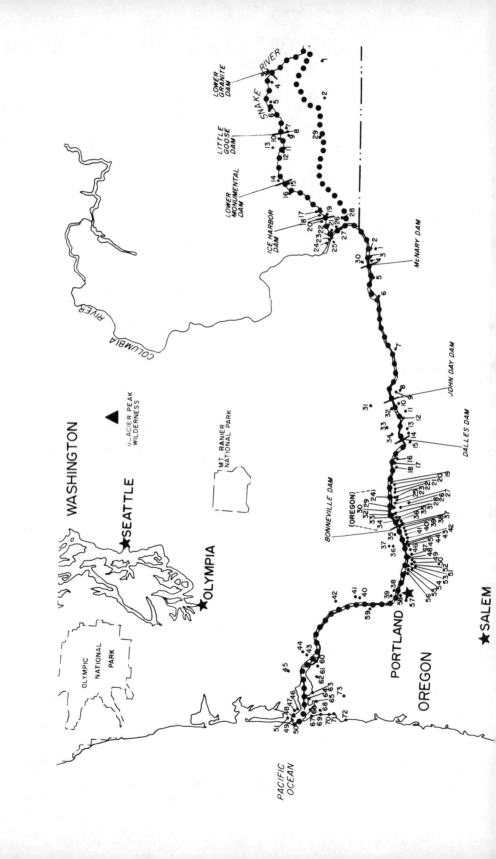

KEY TO THE MAPS

Map Key No.	Name of Area	Ownership*	Camping	Picnicking	Boating	Swimming	Hunting	Fishing	Hiking	Historic	Archeologic
	ILLINOIS										
1	Cahokia Mounds State Park & Museum	S	X	X						X	X
	MISSOURI										
1	*Jefferson National Expansion Memorial†*	F								X	
2	West Alton Recreation Access	F	X	X	X		X	X			
3	Dresser Island Recreation Access	F	X	X	X		X	X			
4	Creve Coeur Lake										
5	Ft. Zumwalt State Historic Site	S	X		X					X	
6	Ft. Zumwalt State Park	S	X	X						X	
7	Babler Park Recreation Area	S	X	X	X	X		X	X	X	
8	Babler State Park	S	X	X					X	X	
9	Rockwoods Reservation & Range (2 units)	S									
10	Rockwoods County Park	C	X	X					X		
11	Rockwoods Lookout Tower	P		X							
12	(See No. 9)										
13	U. Of Missouri Weldon Springs Express Sta.	S									
14	August A. Busch Wildlife Area	S	X	X			X	X	X		
15	Daniel Boone Home	S	X		X		X				
16	Daniel Boone Shrine	P							X	X	
17	Daniel Boone Burial Site	P								X	
18	Reifsnider State Forest	S	X	X			X		X		
19	Warrenton Tower	S	X						X		
20	Daniel Boone State Forest	S	X	X			X		X		
21	Graham Cave State Park	S								X	
22	Mineola Fire Tower	S		X							
23	Reform Tower	S									
24	Fredricksburg Ferry Access	S									
25	Chamois Access (Grindstone Park)	M			X		X	X			
26	Mokane Access (Ordway Park)	S			X		X	X			
27	Bonnots Mill Recreation Access	S			X		X	X			
28	Mari-Osa Delta	S									
29	Moreau—50 Access	S									
30	State Capitol & Historic Sites	S								X	
31	Cedar Creek Recreation Area	F					X				
32	Binder Lake	S		X	X			X			
33	Marion Access (Projecting Cliff Park)	S			X		X	X			
34	Providence Access	S									
35	Boonslick Frontier	S						X	X	X	

* Ownership Symbols: County = C, State = S, Federal = F, Private = P
Municipal = M, Quasi-Public = Q, Tribal = T
† Site directly relating to Lewis and Clark expedition

KEY TO THE MAPS (cont.)

Map Key No.	Name of Area	Ownership*	Camping	Picnicking	Boating	Swimming	Hunting	Fishing	Hiking	Historic	Archeologic
36	Historic City of Franklin	M								X	
37	Taylors' Landing Access	S									
38	Bourgman Access	S									
39	Herriman Hill Access	S									
40	Backwater Access	S									
41	Prairie of Arrows Public Use Area	S			X		X	X			
42	Boonslick State Park	S		X					X	X	
43	Arrow Rock State Park	S	X	X						X	
44	William Ashley Grave	P								X	
45	Lewis Mill Access	S									
46	Sterling Price Community Lake	S		X	X			X			
47	Brunswick Access	S									
48	Fort Orleans	P								X	X
49	Bosworth Access Area	S		X			X	X			
50	Van Meter State Park	S	X	X						X	X
51	Malta Bend Community Lake	S		X				X			
52	Confederate Memorial State Park	S		X				X		X	
53	Civil War Battle of Lexington State Park	S								X	
54	Fort Osage County Park	C		X						X	
55	Kansas City Historic Sites and Parks	M	X	X	X	X		X	X	X	
56	Humphrey Access Recreation Area	S		X							
57	Lewis and Clark Hatchery	S									
58	Lewis and Clark State Park	S	X	X	X			X	X		
59	Pigeon Hill Wildlife Area	S					X				
60	St. Joseph Historic Sites	M								X	
61	Rochester Falls Access Area	S						X			
62	Honey Creek Wildlife Area	S	X	X	X	X	X	X	X		
63	Squaw Creek National Wildlife Refuge	F						X			
64	Big Lake State Park	S	X	X	X	X		X	X		
65	H. F. Thurman Wildlife Area	S					X	X			
66	Brickyard Hill Wildlife Area	F	X	X			X				
	KANSAS										
1	Shawnee Methodist Mission	Q								X	
2	Moses Grinter House	P								X	
3	Huron Cemetery	P								X	
4	Wyandotte County Lake	C	X	X	X	X			X		
5	Fort Leavenworth	F								X	
6	Fred Harvey Home									X	

* Ownership Symbols: County = C, State = S, Federal = F, Private = P
Municipal = M, Quasi-Public = Q, Tribal = T
† Site directly relating to Lewis and Clark expedition

KEY TO THE MAPS (cont.)

Map Key No.	Name of Area	Ownership*	Camping	Picnicking	Boating	Swimming	Hunting	Fishing	Hiking	Historic	Archeologic
						Activities and Attractions					
7	Historic Fort Cavagnal	P								X	
8	Amelia Earhart Birthplace	P								X	
9	Old Priory, St. Benidicts	P								X	
10	Prehistoric Kansa Indian Village	P								X	X
11	Historic Kansa Indian Village	P								X	X
12	Iowa, Sac & Fox Presbyterian Mission	S								X	
13	Irwin Hall, Highland Junior College	P								X	
14	Brown County State Lake	S	X	X	X	X		X	X		
15	Iowa, Sac & Fox Reservations	P								X	
	NEBRASKA										
1	Leary Indian Village Site	P								X	
2	Verdon Lake Recreation Area	S	X	X				X			
3	Brownville Recreation Area	S	X	X	X			X			
4	Historic Brownville	M								X	
5	Otoe County Court House	C								X	
6	Arbor Lodge Historical Park	S								X	
7	Nebraska City Marina	S	X	X	X			X			
8	Plattsmouth Waterfowl Management Area	P		X				X			
9	Oto Indian Mission	P									
10	Historic Bellevue	M								X	X
11	Fontenelle Forest	Q						X	X		
12	Benson Park	M		X							
13	Elmwood Park	M		X							
14	Riverview Park	M		X							
15	Joslyn Art Museum	P								X	
16	Old Florence & Mormon Cemetery	Q								X	
17	Cabanne Trading Post	P								X	
18	Lisa Trading Post	P								X	
19	Historic Council Bluffs	S								X	
20	Blackbird Hill	P								X	
21	Chief Big Elk Recreation Area	P	X	X	X						
22	Big Bear Hollow Recreation Area	P	X	X	X				X		
23	Omadi Bend Recreation	S	X	X	X			X			
24	Omaha Indian Village	P								X	
25	Historic Dakota City	M								X	
26	Crystal Lake Wayside Recreation Area	S	X	X				X			
27	Ponca State Park	S	X	X	X	X			X		
28	Calumet Bluff Council Site	F								X	

* Ownership Symbols: County = C, State = S, Federal = F, Private = P
  Municipal = M, Quasi-Public = Q, Tribal = T
† Site directly relating to Lewis and Clark expedition

KEY TO THE MAPS *(cont.)*

Map Key No.	Name of Area	Ownership*	Camping	Picnicking	Boating	Swimming	Hunting	Fishing	Hiking	Historic	Archeologic
29	Gavins Point Dam & Recreation Areas	F	X	X	X	X		X		X	
30	Weigand Recreation Area	S	X	X	X	X		X			
31	Bloomfield Recreation Area	F	X	X	X						
32	Miller Creek Recreation Area	F		X		X					
33	Santee Recreation Area	F		X				X		X	
34	Niobrara Recreation Area	F		X	X						
35	Niobrara State Park	S	X	X	X	X		X	X	X	
	IOWA										
1	Waubonsie Access	S			X		X	X			
2	Waubonsie State Park	S	X	X					X		
3	Sidney Recreation Area	C	X	X							
4	Riverton Game Management Area						X	X			
5	I-29 Rest Area	C									
6	I-29 Rest Area	S	X	X							
7	Plum Creek	S					X	X			
8	Auldon Bar Island	S						X			
9	Forney's Lake	S					X	X			
10	John Brown and Underground Railroad	M								X	
11	Pinky's Glenn	C									
12	Nottleman Island	S						X			
13	Mills County Historical Building	C								X	
14	Pony Creek Park	C	X	X					X		X
15	Long's Landing	S		X				X			
16	Lake Manawa State Park	S	X	X	X	X	X	X			
17	Gifford Wildlife Sanctuary	S									
18	*Council Bluffs Historic Sites†*	Q								X	
19	Smith Wildlife Refuge	S									
20	Carters Lake	S		X	X	X					
21	Wilson Island Recreation Area	S	X	X	X		X	X			
22	Nobels Lake	S						X			
23	Niles Historic Museum	C								X	
24	DeSota National Wildlife Refuge	F					X	X			
25	Round Lake Recreation Area	S					X	X			
26	Huff Access	C	X	X	X		X	X			
27	Preparation Canyon Recreation Area	S	X	X					X		
28	Monona Arboretum	C		X							
29	Lewis and Clark State Park	S	X	X		X		X			
30	Blue Lake	S					X	X			

* Ownership Symbols: County = C, State = S, Federal = F, Private = P
Municipal = M, Quasi-Public = Q, Tribal = T
† Site directly relating to Lewis and Clark expedition

KEY TO THE MAPS (cont.)

Map Key No.	Name of Area	Ownership*	Camping	Picnicking	Boating	Swimming	Hunting	Fishing	Hiking	Historic	Archeologic
					Activities and Attractions						
31	Onawa Access Recreation Area	S	X				X	X			
32	Loess Hills Wildlife Area	S					X				
33	Decatur Access Recreation Area	S	X				X	X			
34	Brown's Lake State Park	S	X	X	X	X	X	X			
35	Lake Port Twp. Wildlife Area	C					X				
36	Snyder Bend	C	X	X	X	X			X	X	
37	Guernsey Park	C		X	X	X		X			
38	Liberty Twp. Wildlife Area	C					X		X		
39	New Lake	S			X			X	X		
40	*Sergeant Floyd Monument†*	Q								X	
41	Sioux City Historic Sites	M								X	
	SOUTH DAKOTA										
1	Elk Point River Desert	P		X						X	
2	Custer Camp Site	P								X	
3	James River Recreation Area	P								X	
4	Historic Yankton	M								X	
5	Gavins Point National Fish Hatchery	F									
6	Gavins Point Dam & Recreation Areas	F	X	X	X	X		X	X	X	
7	White Bear Cliff	F								X	
8	Lesterville Recreation Area	F						X			
9	Tabor Recreation Area	F	X	X	X						
10	Bon Homme Community	P								X	
11	Sand Creek Recreation Area	F		X	X			X			
12	Historic Springfield	M		X	X					X	
13	Yankton Indian Agency	P								X	
14	Trudeau Cabin	P								X	
15	Old Fort Randall	F								X	
16	Randall Creek Recreation Area	F	X	X	X			X			
17	Fort Randall Dam and Recreation Area	F	X	X	X	X		X	X		
18	Lake Andes National Wildlife Refuge	F						X			
19	South Shore Recreation Area	F		X	X			X			
20	North Point Public Use Area	F	X	X	X	X					
21	Spring Creek Public Use Area	F						X			
22	South Scalp Creek Public Use Area	F						X			
23	North Scalp Creek	F						X			
24	Pease Creek Public Use Area	F			X			X			
25	South Wheeler Public Use Area	F		X	X						
26	North Wheeler Public Use Area	F		X	X			X		X	

* Ownership Symbols: County = C, State = S, Federal = F, Private = P
Municipal = M, Quasi-Public = Q, Tribal = T

† Site directly relating to Lewis and Clark expedition

KEY TO THE MAPS (cont.)

Map Key No.	Name of Area	Ownership*	Camping	Picnicking	Boating	Swimming	Hunting	Fishing	Hiking	Historic	Archeologic
					Activities and Attractions						
27	Whetstone Creek Public Use Areas	F			X	X		X			
28	Stricker Bottom Public Use Area	F	X	X							
29	Platte Creek Public Use Area	F		X	X			X			
30	Platte Public Recreation Area	F						X			
31	Snake Creek Public Use Area	F						X			
32	Turgeon Bottom Public Use Area	F						X			
33	Turgeon Well Public Use Area	F						X			
34	Landing Creek Public Use Area	F	X	X							
35	Elm Creek Public Use Area	F						X			
36	Waterhole Creek Public Use Area	F		X	X			X			
37	Five Mile Public Use Area	F						X			
38	White River Recreation Areas	S									
39	Old Lower Brule Indian Agency	F								X	
40	Chamberlain—West Bank Recreation Area	F			X			X			
41	Chamberlain—American Creek Rec. Area	F			X			X			
42	Kiowa Unit Recreation Area	F					X				
43	Brule Bottom Wildlife Area	F						X			
44	Military Fort Lookout	P								X	
45	Fur Post, Ft. Lookout (Fort Kiowa)	F								X	
46	Old Fort Hale	P								X	
47	Crow Creek Indian Village	F									X
48	Tailwaters Public Use Area	F						X			
49	Big Bend Dam and Recreation Areas	F			X			X			
50	Fort Thompson—Crow Creek Agency	F									
51	Fort Thompson Recreation Area	PF	X	X	X	X					
52	Soldier Creek Public Use Area	F			X			X			
53	Big Bend Overlook	P								X	
54	Jiggs Thompson Indian Village	F									
55	Langdeau Indian Village	F									
56	Counselor Creek	F			X						
57	Lower Brule Indian Agency	F								X	
58	Red Cloud Agency Recreation Area	F	X	X				X			
59	Iron Nation Public Use Area	F			X						
60	West Bend Public Use Area	F			X			X			
61	Joe Creek Public Use Area	F			X			X			
62	Cedar Creek Public Use Area	F			X			X			
63	Loisel's Post	F								X	
64	DeGrey Public Use Area	F			X			X			
65	Chapelle Creek Overlook	P								X	

* Ownership Symbols: County = C, State = S, Federal = F, Private = P
Municipal = M, Quasi-Public = Q, Tribal = T
† Site directly relating to Lewis and Clark expedition

KEY TO THE MAPS *(cont.)*

Map Key No.	Name of Area	Ownership*	Camping	Picnicking	Boating	Swimming	Hunting	Fishing	Hiking	Historic	Archeologic
					Activities and Attractions						
66	Antelope Creek Public Use Area	F			X			X			
67	Prehistoric Indian Village	P								X	X
68	Fort Sully I	P								X	
69	Farm Island Recreation Park	F								X	
70	LaFrambois Island	F		X	X						
71	Verendrye Plaque Discovery Site	S								X	
72	Snake Butte Mosaic	P									X
73	Ft. Pierre Chouteau	P S								X	X
74	Oahe Dam and Recreation Areas	F	X	X	X	X		X	X	X	X
75	Oahe Mission Chapel	S								X	
76	Sully Indian Village	F								X	X
77	Little Bend Overlook	P									
78	Cheyenne River Agency Overlook	F								X	
79	Whitlocks Bay Public Use Area	F			X			X			
80	Indian Creek Public Use Area	F									
81	LeCompte Creek Indian Village									X	X
82	*Sakakawea Monument†*	P								X	
83	Sitting Bull Memorial	P								X	
84	Prehistoric Indian Village	F								X	
85	Sitting Bull Gallery & Museum	M								X	
86	Indian Memorial Public Use Area	F		X	X						
87	Pocasse National Wildlife Refuge	F	X	X	X	X		X			
88	Lake Pocasse Public Use Area	F		X	X	X		X			
	NORTH DAKOTA										
1	Ft. Yates & Standing Rock Indian Agency	T								X	
2	Sitting Bull Monument	S								X	
3	Cretaceous Sandstone Outcrops	P									
4	North Cannonball Indian Village Site										X
5	Fort Rice Historic Site	S								X	
6	Shermer Indian Village										X
7	Huff Indian Village Site	S									X
8	Eagle Nose Indian Village	P C									X
9	Burleigh	F					X	X			
10	Wildlife Management Area (Oahe)	F					X	X			
11	Slant Indian Village Site	S								X	X
12	Fort Lincoln State Park	S	X	X	X			X	X	X	
13	City of Bismarck Recreation Area	CF	X	X	X	X		X	X	X	
14	Camp Hancock Museum	C								X	

* Ownership Symbols: County = C, State = S, Federal = F, Private = P
  Municipal = M, Quasi-Public = Q, Tribal = T
† Site directly relating to Lewis and Clark expedition

KEY TO THE MAPS (cont.)

Activities and Attractions

Map Key No.	Name of Area	Ownership*	Camping	Picnicking	Boating	Swimming	Hunting	Fishing	Hiking	Historic	Archeologic
15	Outcrops of Cannonball Formation	P									
16	Ward Indian Village Site	S									X
17	Rock Haven Historical Site	S								X	
18	Double Ditch Indian Village Site	S								X	X
19	Boley Indian Village Site	S								X	X
20	Lignite Beds—Fossil Shells	P									
21	Larson Indian Village Site	S									X
22	Emmons	F					X	X			
23	Molander Indian Village Site	S								X	X
24	Arroda Lake Game Management Area	S					X				
25	Mandan Lake	S					X	X			
26	*Fort Clark Historic Site†*	S								X	
27	Big White & Black Cat Indian Village Site	S								X	X
28	*Fort Mandan†*	S								X	
29	*Lower Hidatsa Village Site†*	P								X	X
30	*Sakakawea Village Site†*	P								X	X
31	*Big Hidatsa Village Site†*	F								X	X
32	Riverdale Game Management Area	F	X	X				X	X		
33	Garrison Dam National Fish Hatchery	F									
34	Outlet Channel Fishing Camp	F		X				X			
35	Little Missouri Bay State Park	S	X	X				X			
36	Garrison Dam Downstream Public Use Area	F	X	X	X			X			
37	Garrison Reservoir State Park	S	X	X	X	X	X	X	X		
38	Garrison Dam	F						X			
39	Exposed Coal Beds in Tongue Formation	F									
40	Wolf Creek Public Use Area	F	X	X	X			X			
41	Wolf Creek Game Management Area	F					X	X			
42	Snake Creek National Wildlife Refuge	F		X			X	X			
43	Snake Creek Game Management Area	F	X	X	X		X	X			
44	Totten Trail Public Use Area	F	X	X	X		X	X			
45	Fort Stevenson Public Use Area	F	X	X	X			X			
46	Garrison Game Management Area	F					X	X			
47	Douglas Creek Public Use Area	F	X	X	X			X			
48	Douglas Creek Game Management Area	F	X				X	X			
49	Hille Game Management Area	F					X	X			
50	Beulah Bay Public Use Area	F	X	X				X			
51	Custer's Ree Scouts' Cemetery	P		X						X	
52	Beaver Creek Game Management Area	F						X			
53	Beaver Creek Fishing Camp	F		X				X			

* Ownership Symbols: County = C, State = S, Federal = F, Private = P
Municipal = M, Quasi-Public = Q, Tribal = T
† Site directly relating to Lewis and Clark expedition

Activities and Attractions

Map Key No.	Name of Area	Ownership*	Camping	Picnicking	Boating	Swimming	Hunting	Fishing	Hiking	Historic	Archeologic
54	Little Shell Creek Fishing Camp	F		X				X			
55	Nishu Bay Fishing Camp	F		X				X			
56	Twin Buttes Recreational Area	F		X	X						
57	*Hidatsa Village Site†*	P	X								
58	Red Butte Bay Public Use Area	F	X	X	X						
59	Mandan "Big Canoe" Shrine	P								X	
60	Seven Rocks	P								X	
61	Halliday Public Use Area	M	X	X	X			X			
62	Saddle Butte Bay Recreation Area	P	X					X			
63	Deepwater Creek Game Management Area	F					X	X			
64	Deepwater Creek Public Use Area	F	X	X			X				
65	Van Hook Game Management Area	F					X	X			
66	Shell Creek Bay	PM	X	X	X	X		X			
67	Skunk Creek Fishing Camp			X				X			
68	Reunion Point Fishing Camp	F		X				X			
69	Two Moon Bay	F		X	X			X			
70	Bear Den Recreation Area	P	X	X				X			
71	Hunts Along Bay	F		X	X			X			
72	Four Bears Park	P	X	X	X	X		X	X	X	
73	New Town Fishing Camp	F		X				X			
74	Hall's Trading Post Fishing Camp	F		X				X			
75	Crow Flies High Butte	S								X	
76	Tobacco Garden Creek Public Use Area	F	X	X	X			X			
77	Tobacco Garden Game Management Area	F					X	X			
78	Lewis and Clark Public Use Area	F	X	X	X			X			
79	Henry's Post	S								X	
80	Fort Buford Historic Park	S		X					X	X	
81	Fort Union Historic Site	S								X	
	MONTANA										
1	*Lewis and Clark Memorial Park†*	M	X	X	X	X	X	X	X		
2	Rock Creek State Recreation Area	F	X	X	X	X		X			
3	Bear Creek Public Use Area	F		X	X			X			
4	Fort Peck Downstream Public Use Area	F	X	X	X	X		X			
5	Fort Peck Game Station	F	X		X			X			
6	Fort Peck Exhibition Pasture	F									
7	Fort Peck Public Use Area	F	X	X	X			X			
8	The Pines Public Use Area	F	X	X	X	X		X			
9	Hell Creek State Recreation Area	F	X	X	X	X		X			

* Ownership Symbols: County = C, State = S, Federal = F, Private = P
         Municipal = M, Quasi-Public = Q, Tribal = T
† Site directly relating to Lewis and Clark expedition

Activities and Attractions

Map Key No.	Name of Area	Ownership*	Camping	Picnicking	Boating	Swimming	Hunting	Fishing	Hiking	Historic	Archeologic
10	Devil's Creek Public Use Area	F	X	X			X	X			
11	Slippery Ann Game Station	F							X		
12	James Kipp State Recreation Area	F	X	X	X			X			
13	Bighorn Sheep Pasture	F							X		
14	Cow Island Recreation Area	S	X	X	X		X	X		X	
15	Judith Landing Recreation Area†	S	X	X	X		X	X		X	
16	Slaughter River Recreation Area	S	X	X	X		X	X		X	
17	Hole-in-the-Wall Recreation Area	S	X	X	X		X	X		X	
18	Citadel Rock State Monument†	S									
19	Coal Banks Landing Recreation Area	S	X	X	X		X	X		X	
20	Tiber Reservoir Recreation Area	F	X	X	X	X	X	X	X		
21	Carter Ferry Fishing Access Site	S						X			
22	Ryan Island Picnic Area	P		X							
23	Giant Spring Picnic Area†	M		X				X			
24	Holter Lake Recreation Area	F	X	X	X	X	X	X	X		
25	Holter Lake Picnic Area	P		X	X						
26	Beartooth Game Range	S	X	X	X	X	X	X	X		
27	Meriwether Picnic Area	F		X	X				X	X	
28	Gates of the Mountain Wild Area†	F	X				X	X	X		
29	Canyon Ferry Recreation Area	F	X	X	X	X	X	X	X	X	
30	Fairweather Fishing Access Site	S					X	X			
31	Missouri River Headwaters State Monument†	S	X	X			X			X	
32	Williams Bridge Fishing Access Site	S						X			
33	Harrison Lake Access Site	S	X		X			X			
34	Lewis and Clark Caverns State Park	S	X	X							
35	Cardwell Fishing Access Site	S						X			
36	Beaverhead Rock	P									
37	Barretts Diversion Dam Recreation Area	F	X	X			X	X		X	
38	Clark Canyon Reservoir Recreation Area†	F	X	X	X	X		X		X	
39	Willards Pass	F							X		
40	Bannock State Monument	S	X	X			X			X	
41	Sacajawea Memorial Area†	F		X						X	
42	Big Hole National Battlefield Monument	F								X	
43	Lost Trail Visitor Center†	F								X	
44	Lost Trail Ski Area	F									
45	Indian Tree Campground	F	X	X						X	
46	Warm Springs Campground	F	X	X							
47	Spring Gulch Campground	F	X	X							
48	Hannon Memorial Fishing Access Site	S						X			

* Ownership Symbols: County = C, State = S, Federal = F, Private = P
  Municipal = M, Quasi-Public = Q, Tribal = T
† Site directly relating to Lewis and Clark expedition

KEY TO THE MAPS (cont.)

	Name of Area	Ownership*	Camping	Picnicking	Boating	Swimming	Hunting	Fishing	Hiking	Historic	Archeologic
					Activities and Attractions						
49	Durland Park			X							
50	Lake Como Campground	F	X	X	X	X					
51	Bitterroot Game Range	S					X				
52	Blodgett Park			X							
53	Fort Owen State Monument	S								X	
54	*Travelers Rest†*	C									
55	Bass Creek Recreation Area	F	X	X							
56	Florence Bridge Fishing Access Site	S		X				X			
57	Chief Looking Glass Fishing Access Site	S	X	X				X			
58	Van Buren Bridge										
59	Nine Mile Prairie Fishing Access Site	S						X			
60	Clearwater Crossing Fishing Access Site	S	X	X				X		X	
61	Blackfoot-Clearwater Game Range	S					X	X			
62	Upsata Lake Fishing Access	S						X			
63	Montvue Fishing Access Site	S	X	X				X			
64	River Junction Fishing Access Site	S						X			
65	Harry Morgan Fishing Access Site	S						X			
66	Blackfoot Campground	F	X	X				X			
67	Hooper State Recreation Area	S	X	X							
68	Aspen Grove Campground	F	X	X				X			
69	Bean Lake Fishing Access Site	S	X	X	X			X			
70	Sun River Game Range	S					X				
71	Willow Creek National Wildlife Refuge	F	X	X	X			X			
72	Madison Buffalo Jump State Monument	S								X	X
73	Four Corners Fishing Access Site	S						X			
74	Sheep Mountain Fishing Access	S		X				X			
75	Grey Bear Fishing Access Site	S	X	X	X		X	X		X	
76	Bratton Fishing Access Site										
77	Indian Fort Fishing Access Site	S	X	X	X		X	X			
78	Swinging Bridge Fishing Access Site	S						X			
79	Itch-Kep-Pe Fishing Access Site	S						X			
80	Sportsman's Park	P									
81	Pictograph Cave State Monument	S		X							X
82	*Pompeys Pillar†*	P		X				X	X	X	
83	Rosebud Recreation Area	S	X	X	X			X			
84	Brannum Lake Fishing Access Site	S		X				X			
85	Spotted Eagle Recreation Area	P									
86	Makoshika State Park	S	X	X							
87	Intake Dam Fishing Access Site	S	X	X	X						

* Ownership Symbols: County = C, State = S, Federal = F, Private = P
Municipal = M, Quasi-Public = Q, Tribal = T
† Site directly relating to Lewis and Clark expedition

KEY TO THE MAPS (cont.)

Activities and Attractions

Map Key No.	Name of Area	Ownership*	Camping	Picnicking	Boating	Swimming	Hunting	Fishing	Hiking	Historic	Archeologic
88	*Lewis and Clark Campground†*	F	X	X							
89	Lee Creek Campground	F	X	X							
	IDAHO										
1	*Sacajawea Recreational Area†*	F								X	
2	Agency Creek Campground	F	X	X							
3	Lemhi Power Site Access Site	S						X			
4	Salmon Access Site	S						X			
5	Salmon River—Belander Access Site	S						X			
6	Wagonhammer Spring Picnic Area	F		X						X	
7	Twin Creeks Campground	F	X	X							
8	State Creek Campground	F	X								
9	*Lost Trail Pass Recreation Area†*	F	X	X							
10	Bernard DeVoto Memorial Grove	F								X	
11	Whitesand Campground	F	X	X							
12	Powell Campground	F	X	X			X	X			
13	Whitehouse Campground	F	X	X				X			
14	Wendover Campground	F	X	X				X			
15	Jerry Johnson Campground	F	X	X							
16	Green Flat Campground	F	X	X				X			
17	Wilderness Gateway Campground	F	X				X	X			
18	Major Fenn Picnic Ground	F		X				X			
19	*Glade Creek Campground†*	F	X	X				X			
20	Apgar Campground	F	X	X				X			
21	Wild Goose Campground	F	X	X	X			X			
22	Three Devils Picnic Ground	F		X	X			X			
23	Brown's Ridge Recreation Site	F		X						X	
24	Tom Taha Creek Recreation Site	F	X	X							
25	*Nez Perce National Historical Park*										
	(E. Kamiah Unit)†	F								X	
26	Saw Shop Hole Access Site	S		X				X			
27	Dworshak Fish Hatchery	F									
28	Dworshak Dam Visitor Facility	F		X							
29	Big Eddy Boat Launching Area	F		X	X				X		
30	*Nez Perce National Historical Park*										
	(Canoe Camp)†	F		X						X	
31	Big Canyon Access Site	S		X				X			
32	Lenore Access Site	S		X				X			
33	Cherry Lane Access Site	S		X				X			

* Ownership Symbols: County = C, State = S, Federal = F, Private = P
                Municipal = M, Quasi-Public = Q, Tribal = T
† Site directly relating to Lewis and Clark expedition

KEY TO THE MAPS *(cont.)*

Activities and Attractions

Map Key No.	Name of Area	Ownership*	Camping	Picnicking	Boating	Swimming	Hunting	Fishing	Hiking	Historic	Archeologic
34	Myrtle Beach Access Site	S			X			X			
35	Clearwater No. 2 Recreation Site	F	X	X							
36	Spalding Road Access Site	S			X			X			
37	Nez Perce National Historical Park										
	(Spalding Site)	F		X						X	
38	Hatwai Creek Access Site	S						X			
39	Lewiston Levi Parkways	F		X					X	X	
40	Hell's Gate State Recreation Area	F	X	X	X	X		X	X		X
	WASHINGTON										
1	Asotin Game Range	S	X				X				
2	W. T. Wooten Game Range	S	X				X	X			
3	Boyer Park and Marina	F		X	X			X			
4	Lilia Landing	F		X	X			X			
5	Willow Landing	F		X				X			
6	Central Ferry State Park	F		X				X			
7	Little Goose Landing	F		X	X	X					
8	Little Goose Lock & Dam	F									
9	Texas Rapids Recreation Site	F	X	X	X			X			
10	Riparia	F		X				X			
11	*Lyons Ferry State Park†*	F	X	X	X	X		X	X	X	X
12	Lyons Ferry Marina	F	X	X	X			X			
13	Palouse Falls State Park	S	X	X							
14	Lower Monumental Dam	F									
15	Matthews	F		X				X			
16	Windust Park	F	X	X				X			
17	Big Flat	F	X	X							
18	Levey Landing Park	F	X	X	X			X			
19	*Charbonneau Park†*	F	X	X	X						
20	Ice Harbor Dam	F									
21	Hood Park	F	X	X	X						
22	*Sacajawea State Park†*	SF	X	X	X			X		X	
23	Pasco Boat Basin	F	X	X							
24	Chiawana Park	F	X	X	X						
25	Columbia Park	F	X	X	X	X		X	X		
26	McNary National Wildlife Refuge	F						X			
27	McNary Game Range	F		X			X	X			
28	Wallula Park	F		X	X						
29	*Lewis and Clark Trail State Park†*	S	X	X				X			

* Ownership Symbols: County = C, State = S, Federal = F, Private = P
 Municipal = M, Quasi-Public = Q, Tribal = T
† Site directly relating to Lewis and Clark expedition

KEY TO THE MAPS *(cont.)*

Activities and Attractions

Map Key No.	Name of Area	Ownership*	Camping	Picnicking	Boating	Swimming	Hunting	Fishing	Hiking	Historic	Archeologic
30	McNary Dam	F									
31	Brooks Memorial State Park	S	X	X							
32	Maryhill Park	F		X	X	X					
33	Avery Recreation Area	F		X	X	X		X			
34	Horsethief Lake State Park	F		X	X	X		X			
35	Beacon Rock State Park	S	X	X	X			X	X	X	
36	Skamania Hatchery	S									
37	Washougal Salmon Hatchery	S									
38	Vancouver Hatchery	S									
39	Fort Vancouver National Historic Site	F								X	
40	Paradise Point State Park	S	X	X	X	X		X			
41	Lewis River Salmon Hatchery	S									
42	Kalama Salmon Hatchery	S									
43	Beaver Creek Hatchery	S									
44	Elokomin Salmon Hatchery	S									
45	Grays River Salmon Hatchery	S									
46	Fort Columbia State Park	S		X				X		X	
47	*Lewis and Clark Campsite State Park†*	S								X	
48	Chinook Small-Boat Basin	M			X			X			
49	Ilwaco Small-Boat Basin	M			X			X			
50	Fort Canby State Park; Lewis & Clark Interpretative Center	S	X	X			X			X	
51	Willapa National Wildlife Refuge	F					X				
	OREGON										
1	Cold Springs National Wildlife Refuge	F	X				X				
2	Hat Rock State Park	SF		X	X	X		X	X	X	
3	McNary Beach Park	F		X		X					
4	Umatilla Park & Marina	F	X	X	X	X					
5	Irrigon Park	F		X	X	X					
6	Boardman Park	F		X	X	X					
7	Arlington Park	F		X	X	X					
8	Phillipi Park	F		X	X	X		X			
9	LePage Park	F	X	X	X	X			X	X	
10	Biggs Recreation Area	F						X			
11	Deschutes River State Recreation Area	S	X	X	X	X		X			
12	Celilo Park	F		X	X	X		X		X	
13	The Dalles Viewpoint and Memorial	F								X	
14	Seufert Park	F								X	X

* Ownership Symbols: County = C, State = S, Federal = F, Private = P
Municipal = M, Quasi-Public = Q, Tribal = T
† Site directly relating to Lewis and Clark expedition

KEY TO THE MAPS *(cont.)*

Activities and Attractions

Map Key No.	Name of Area	Ownership*	Camping	Picnicking	Boating	Swimming	Hunting	Fishing	Hiking	Historic	Archeologic
15	The Dalles Small-Boat Basin	M			X						
16	Mayer State Park	S		X	X	X		X			
17	Memaloose State Park	S		X						X	
18	Koberg Beach State Wayside	S		X	X	X		X			
19	Hood River Small-Boat Basin	M			X						
20	Seneca Fouts Memorial State Park	S							X		
21	Vinzenz Lausmann Memorial State Park	S							X		
22	Wygant State Park	S		X					X		
23	Starvation Creek State Park	S		X					X	X	
24	Viento State Park	S	X	X				X			
25	Old Wagon Road Historical Area	F								X	
26	Hood River Trout Hatchery	S									
27	Lindsey Creek State Park	S							X		
28	Herman Creek Campground	F	X	X					X		
29	Wyeth Development Site	F	X	X							
30	Long State Park	S									
31	Oxbow Salmon Hatchery	S									
32	Cascade Locks Marine Park	M	X	X	X			X	X		
33	Cascade Locks Indian Picnic Site	F		X				X		X	
34	Sheridan State Park	S								X	
35	Overlook Picnic Ground	F		X							
36	Cascade Salmon Hatchery	S									
37	Eagle Creek Picnic Ground	F	X	X					X		
38	Bonneville Salmon Hatchery	S									
39	Bonneville State Park	S									
40	John B. Yeon State Park	S						X			
41	McLoughlin State Park	S							X		
42	Ainsworth State Park	S	X	X				X			
43	Multnomah Falls Lodge	F							X		
44	Benson State Park	S		X	X	X		X			
45	Wahkenna Falls Picnic Ground	F		X					X		
46	Shepperd's Dell State Park								X		
47	George W. Joseph State Park	S							X		
48	Rooster Rock State Park	S		X	X	X		X		X	
49	Guy W. Talbot State Park	S		X					X		
50	Crown Point State Park	S									
51	Oxbow Park	CSF	X	X		X		X	X		
52	Portland Women's Forum State Park	S									
53	Dabney State Park	S		X		X		X	X		

* Ownership Symbols: County = C, State = S, Federal = F, Private = P
Municipal = M, Quasi-Public = Q, Tribal = T
† Site directly relating to Lewis and Clark expedition

KEY TO THE MAPS (cont.)

Activities and Attractions

Map Key No.	Name of Area	Ownership*	Camping	Picnicking	Boating	Swimming	Hunting	Fishing	Hiking	Historic	Archeologic
54	*Lewis and Clark State Park*†	S	X	X	X	X		X		X	
55	Blue Lake Park	C		X	X	X		X			
56	Government Island Game Management Area	S		X	X		X	X			
57	Oregon Slough Entrance Channel	P			X			X			
58	Willamette Stone State Park	S							X	X	
59	Sauvie Island Game Management Area	S		X	X		X	X			
60	Bradley State Wayside	S		X							
61	Gnat Creek Fish Hatchery	S									
62	Big Creek Salmon Hatchery	S									
63	John Day River Park	C		X	X	X		X		X	
64	Astoria Small-Boat Basin	M			X			X			
65	*Fort Clatsop*†	F		X						X	
66	Warrenton Small-Boat Basin	M			X			X			
67	Fort Stevens State Park	F	X	X	X	X		X	X	X	
68	Cullaby Lake Park	C		X	X	X		X	X		
69	Del Rey Beach State Wayside	S				X		X	X		
70	Gearhart Ocean Wayside	S				X		X	X		
71	*Salt Cairn, Seaside*†	P								X	
72	*Ecola State Park*†	S		X	X		X	X		X	X
73	Saddle Mountain State Park	S	X	X					X		

* Ownership Symbols: County = C, State = S, Federal = F, Private = P
    Municipal = M, Quasi-Public = Q, Tribal = T
† Site directly relating to Lewis and Clark expedition

A Selection of Drawings and Entries in Longhand from the Lewis and Clark Journals

Christmas
Wednesday 25th December 1805 76

at day light this morning we we[re] awoke by the discharge of the fire arm of all our party as a Selute, Shouts and a Song which the whole party joined in under our windows, after which they retired to their rooms were Cheerfull all the morning   after brackfast we divided our Tobacco which amounted to 12 carrots one half of which we gave to the men of the party who used tobacco, and to those who doe not use it we make a present of a hand-kerchief, The Indians leave us in the evening. all the party Snugly fixed in their hutts. I recved a present of Capt L. of a fleece hosrie Shirt Draws and Socks., a pr Mockersons of Whitehouse a Small Indian basket of Gutherich, two Dozen white weazils tails of the Indian woman, & some black root of the Indians before their Departure. Drewyer informs me that he Saw a Snake pass across the parth to day. This day proved Showerey wet and disagreeable.

we would have Spent this day the nativity of Christ in feasting, had we any thing either to raise our Spirits or even gratify our appetites, our Diner Consisted of pore Elk, so much Spoiled that we eate it thro' mear necessity, Some Spoiled pounded fish and a fiew roots.

A page from Captain Clark's journal in which he describes Christmas, 1805, at Fort Clatsop

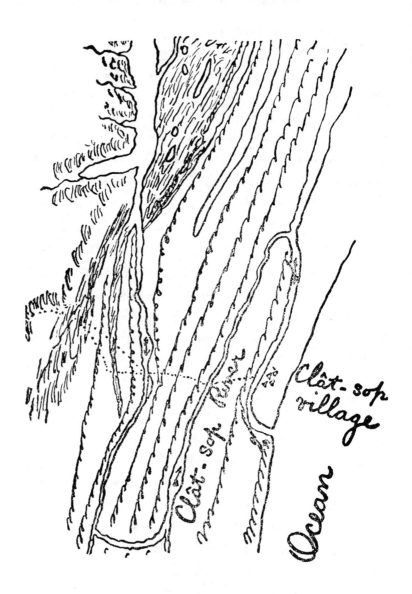

Clark's map of the salt cairn site at present-day Seaside, Oregon

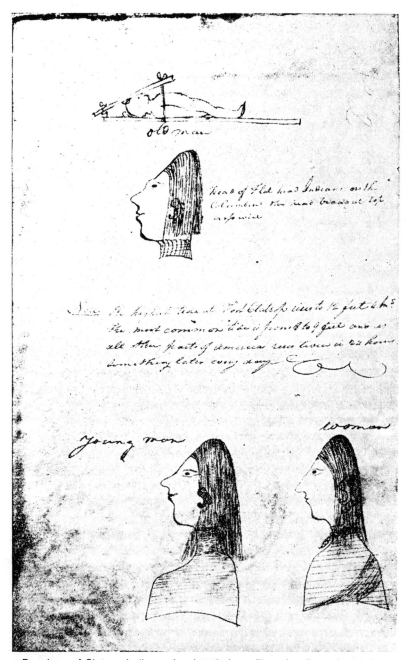

Drawings of Clatsop Indians, showing their profiles after flattening their heads, and how the flattening was accomplished

During the long winter of 1805-06, the captains had ample time to work on their journals and field notes, and they made more drawings then than at any other period of their journey. This page has a drawing of a salmon with descriptive text surrounding it.

Index

Index

Index

Index

8667370